ALICE SQUINTED HAPPILY AT HER NEW COMPANION.

"I'M ALICE! MY FRIENDS HERE ARE BONEY AND BUBBLY. WE'RE SO HAPPY TO HAVE YOU!"

Alice

Member of the Ryota Family.
Able to recruit monsters.

"AND THIS ONE...
IS A WEIRD SHAPE!"
"...A MAGATAMA."
"MAGATAMA?"
Nihonium
The spirit of the dungeon
Nihonium?

ALICE COCKED HER HEAD IN CONFUSION. I NODDED BACK. THE PHYSICAL MIRROR I'D PREVIOUSLY HELD, ALONG WITH THE HOLOGRAM-LIKE SWORD AND MAGATAMA, REMINDED ME OF SOMETHING... THE PHRASE THREE SACRED TREASURES POPPED INTO MY MIND—PERHAPS BECAUSE THIS DUNGEON WAS NIHONIUM, THE ELEMENT NAMED AFTER JAPAN.

Ryota Sato

Bearer of a unique skill. Founder of the Ryota Family.

Emily

Member of the Ryota Family. Has the uncanny power to make places that soothe people.

MY UNIQUE SKILL MAKES ME OP EVEN AT LEVEL 1

4

By Nazuna Miki

Illustrations by Subachi

Translated by Benjamin Daughety

KODANSHA

My Unique Skill Makes Me OP Even at Level 1, 4

A VERTICAL Book

Translation: Benjamin Daughety
Editor: Maneesh Maganti
Production: Shirley Fang
Proofreading: Kevin Luo

Publication rights for this English edition arranged through Kodansha, Ltd., Tokyo.
English language version produced by Kodansha USA Publishing, LLC, 2023.

Originally published in Japan as *Reberu 1 dakedo Yuniiku Sukiru de Saikyou desu 4* by Kodansha, Ltd., Tokyo, 2018.

ISBN 978-1-64729-311-6

Printed in the United States of America

First Edition

Kodansha USA Publishing, LLC
451 Park Avenue South, 7th Floor
New York, NY 10016
www.kodansha.us

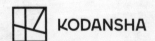 KODANSHA

CONTENTS

009 92. Welcome to the Room of Death

016 93. Unexpected Windfalls

023 94. Two Bullet Hells

031 95. To Go Even Further Beyond

037 96. You Are the Third

044 97. Bomberdemon

050 98. An Unusual Drop

058 99. Limitless

067 100. My Unique Skill Makes Dungeons Grow Even at Level 1

076 101. Unearned Income

082 102. Bank Accounts and Health Bars

087 103. Half the Usual

095 104. Using, But Not Losing

101 105. More Taxes, Less Taxes

109 106. Time for a Career Change

117 107. Part-Timer at Heart

125 108. Two Families

132 109. A Princess's Love

140 110. New Personal Best

146 111. Farming Magic

154 112. New High-Water Mark

158 113. Not Alone

168 114. Limit Break!

174 115. Orange Splitting

180 116. He Who Predicted SS Speed

186 117. The Immovable Object

194 118. Limitless Recovery Rounds

199 119. In a Thousand Years

206 119.5. My True Desire

92.
Welcome to the
Room of Death

I went into B1 of Aurum alone, where I wandered and mowed down little demons. Once I'd traced the unfamiliar passages back to the entrance, I spotted Alice standing out front.

"Sorry for the wait," I said.

"Can I just walk right in?" she asked.

"Yeah."

Alice came into the dungeon, pushing the magic cart all the while.

The surroundings suddenly changed like a scene transition from an old video tape, and we were taken to a place separate from the dungeon entrance we'd just been in.

"No matter how many times it happens, I still can't get used to that," I mused.

"Yeah. It really surprises you, huh?" Alice agreed. She'd been warped away alongside me.

Aurum was a rogue dungeon that changed shape whenever someone entered, after all. If you wanted to fight through it as a party, you had to either all go in and meet up, or go in alone, return to the entrance, and be warped again alongside the next person.

It was a pretty annoying dungeon, in my opinion.

"So, do you feel it?" I asked as I took the magic cart.

Alice confidently pointed and declared, "Yeah! This way."

Ahead and behind us were plain dungeon passages, making it impossible to tell where we'd been taken. And yet, Alice led the way without hesitation.

"So it works? Say, what does that feel like?"

"'That'? What do you mean?"

"How does it feel to just *know* the layout of a dungeon?"

Alice had a special ability: she intuitively knew the layouts and locations of monsters in dungeons.

My hypothesis was that it was caused by her being born inside a dungeon, but at this point, I had no evidence. All we knew was that she could do it.

"I dunno. It's just…a feeling."

"A feeling?"

"Yep, a feeling—oh, a monster's being born!"

Alice stood still and glared forward.

"Hmm?"

I hid behind the magic cart, whipped out my guns, and aimed them ahead. We then waited for a while.

"…No monsters here," I said after a while.

"Just a second… There it is!"

Up ahead, the ceiling broke, and from it emerged a single little demon. It was as if the dungeon itself had given birth to it. After the little demon appeared, the break in the ceiling disappeared, and it became a normal ceiling again.

I fired a normal bullet. Even newborn monsters were still monsters, and this one could already exhibit its full power. It dodged the bullet with ease.

Already assuming that it would do that, I ran forward and cornered it in the direction that it moved. Then, I followed up with a telephone punch.

My punch landed smack-dab in the spot where the demon

was going, launching it into a wall where it stuck. The monster groaned in pain. It was still alive.

Bang! Bang! Bang!

I fired multiple shots at the hole in the wall until there was a *pop*, and the monster disappeared. In its place, a single grain of gold fell, which I picked up.

"That was awesome, Ryota! You were totally merciless."

"Oh yeah?"

"Yeah! It was super cool when you buried it in the wall and went, bang bang!" Alice mimicked.

"The trick to long farming sessions is finishing things off the instant you're able to."

"Oooh, okay, okay! I'll remember that."

She nodded vigorously, taking my advice in. Meanwhile, I entered the value of gold into the magic cart and placed the grain inside. *2,567 piros* appeared right away.

"Oooh. So that's the value of just a grain?"

"It's gold, after all. A piece as big as the space between your pinky's last joint and tip should be worth tens of thousands."

"Wowww! Boney and Bubbly, do you think we could beat them, too?" she asked the chibi skeleton and slime on her shoulders. They moved, answering her in some way. "Oh, okay. We'll have to get more friends, then!"

"Did they say no?"

"Yeah. They said they'd need more help."

"I see."

With that, we continued through the dungeon together. I killed every last little demon along the way. I mean, how could I let any go? Each gram of gold drops was worth about 3,500 piros.

By the time we got to the staircase, we already had 58,121 piros on hand. That alone was worth more than a full cart of bean

sprouts, yet when I looked into the cart, there was only a tiny little pile inside.

"This is awesome! How much do you think we'd make if we filled the whole cart with gold?"

"Hundreds of millions? Billions, even? It's a lot more per gram than veggies, and since they're just grains, we can put a lot more in."

"Whaaat?! Is it really that much?"

"Sure is."

It would be worth that much if we could gather enough, but of course, that was unlikely. Even I would need a full month of mad grinding to get a full cart at this pace, since it takes time to fill a big box when you're going one grain at a time.

Still, the value was insane even without filling the cart, so there wasn't any need to fill it all the way.

"So, on to the next floor?" I suggested.

"Sure! Oh, but there's a monster right next to the bottom of the stairs."

"I'll go down first, then. When it's dead, I'll give the signal."

"Okay!"

I loaded all kinds of bullets to be prepared for any situation, gripped my guns tight, and walked down the stairs to B2 of Aurum.

The moment I stepped inside, the environment blurred.

Does it change shape when you move floors, too?!

Before I knew it, I was in a big chamber. It was like a gymnasium full of monsters.

The monsters themselves were little demons like those on B1, but they had different coloring. Like a second-player color scheme, almost.

And the place was *teeming* with them—just one glance told me they numbered in the three digits.

The phrase *monster house* came to mind.

A fist-sized orb of light flew at me. I guarded right away, but it felt as though I'd been hit by a dodgeball all over.

It didn't stop there, though; all of the monsters attacked at once. In the open gymnasium-like space, orbs of light flew from all directions. Similar impacts struck me over and over, filling my vision with light.

I ended up curling into a turtle-like stance. Since I couldn't see and there were too many of them to dodge, I decided that weathering the storm was my only option. Fortunately, each strike wasn't too bad. Being hit by dodgeballs over and over might sting and make you go numb, but they wouldn't lead to major injuries.

I guarded and occasionally fired recovery rounds into myself just in case, withstanding the onslaught of light orbs. After a while—who knows how long, since my sense of the passage of time was paralyzed by the bizarreness of it all—the number of light orbs decreased.

I looked up and held my guns out. There was a little demon nearby who swung its arm down and attacked with an orb of light.

I guarded and tried to counterattack, but for some reason, the little demon fell and died before I could.

There was an explosive sound as if it had hit something in midair, and it fell to the ground.

What's going on here?

Another orb of light came from my side. I took the blow and pointed my guns that way, but the demon that had attacked also fell to the ground.

Now that I looked around, I realized that the more than hundred demons from before in this monster house had halved in number. The remaining ones were flickering red, too.

Flickering red... Oh!

I took out the slime's tear from my pouch; it was flickering red as well.

The slime's tear, dropped by the high-guts slime outsiders, had two effects: it could trace enemies that I'd attacked, and it could reflect damage.

I stood still, holding it in my hands.

Another orb of light rushed toward me. The instant it struck true, one little demon fell over.

They fired orbs, struck me, and died themselves.

I did nothing but stand there. After three more minutes of that...

"Is it over...?" I mumbled as I surveyed the gymnasium-like chamber.

All of the monsters here had died from damage reflection. In their places were gleaming objects on the ground.

"Gold grains on B2 too, huh?

I began collecting the fallen items. It seemed they dropped gold dust on this floor, too. The monster house had worried me for a moment, but I sized up the amount to be about 300,000 piros, so that was pretty good for doing nothing.

After that, I met up with Alice and we thoroughly searched B2. By the time we were done, the sun was setting.

A day's worth of gold dust turned out to be about a million piros.

93.

Unexpected Windfalls

In front of the dungeon, villagers gathered and watched while Ina, who was on an impromptu loan from the Swallow's Returned Favor, counted the total within the magic cart.

She took the gold dust out and weighed it. Once she'd finished, another employee brought her a safe, from which she counted money and handed it to me.

"Your total comes out to… 1,022,134 piros."

As they witnessed the most orthodox productive activity in this world—the selling of monster drops—the villagers cheered.

"Oooh!"

"So this is how you make money?"

"I like how quickly you get the cash!"

"I'm gonna go in that dungeon tomorrow, too!"

They were impressed and excited.

Once I'd finished selling my drops, the villager Alan took my place in front of Ina.

"T-Take these, too, please."

He requested that she assess the gold dust that he'd gotten from his own delves into Aurum.

"This adds up to 24,932 piros," she replied.

"Oooh…" Alan shuddered with emotion as he received the cash.

A few more people who'd gone into the dungeon sold their drops. Production of goods in dungeons, the sale of item drops from monsters…it was all an everyday thing to me, but the people who'd been waiting so long for a dungeon to appear in their village cheered every time a person finished selling.

With this, the people of Indole learned the entire process from dungeon drop to item sale.

Now, next up…

I asked the girl standing next to me, "Alice, does this village have alcohol? I'd like a lot."

"Alcohol? Hmm… Carlon, Mirau, and the chief might have some. They stock it up for a big festival every year."

"For a festival? Then that ought to do. Could this much money buy it all?" I asked as I showed Alice the million piros we'd earned today.

"Yeah, I think…?"

But why? her curious look seemed to ask.

"It's a big day. Why don't we use this money to host a feast?"

"Oh, we could never!" a woman cut in from behind. She was an old lady, probably about 70, who walked with a cane.

"Who are you?"

"My name is Mirau."

"Oh! Alice said you stock up on alcohol?"

"That's right. If our savior wants to throw a feast, we would be more than happy to let you use our stock."

"Thank you. Then I'll—"

"But we can't take money," she interrupted me. "Not from you."

When she said it, several other villagers piped up in agreement, "Yeah, she's right!"

I appreciated the sentiment, but that would defeat the point.

"Thank you for the thought, but I'd like you to take the

money."

"No, not from our savior…"

"No payment, no feast," I declared outright.

Mirau frowned for a moment, but I wouldn't budge. Eventually, she accepted the money.

"Very well. If that is your wish, savior."

Word got around to Carlon and the chief. They likewise tried to deny the money, but I made them take it.

The village alcohol was cheap, so there was money left over. I entrusted the rest to the chief to use on food for the feast.

While villagers began working to prepare for the feast, Alice came to my side and asked, "Hey, Ryota? Why were you so stubborn about paying them?"

"A long time ago, I went on this business trip overseas for half a year. It took me to a village a lot like this one."

"Huh?" Alice cocked her head, even more confused now.

You might not understand now, but I think you will soon enough.

While the banquet in the village plaza raged on and Ryota drank alongside the villagers, Mirau summoned a villager named Rei and spoke to him in the corner of the plaza.

"Yes, Old Lady Mirau?" Rei asked.

"Rei, your carpentry skills are still up to snuff, aren't they?"

"Of course. Need house repairs?"

"Oh, nobody cares about a house inhabited by an old hag like me. I want to build a new home behind mine. When my son heard a dungeon had formed here, he said he'd come home."

"Hey, that's great news!"

"Thanks to our savior's big spending on the alcohol, I presume this will be enough?" Mirau handed Rei a paper bill.

"Just so you know, this'll only pay for my labor."

"I know that. I have the material cost ready, and I'll order it tomorrow."

"Job accepted. Leave it to me; I'll build something nice for your son."

Rei put the money in his pocket, and Mirau trudged back to the party with her cane.

"Reeei!"

"Whoa?! Geez, Lecia, don't scare me like that."

"Ahem!"

The middle-aged woman named Lecia held out her hand to Rei.

"Wh-What?"

"Don't play dumb; I saw that. You made money, so pay your tab."

"Y-You're gonna take this? But if you take it all, I…"

"Pay what you owe. You can always run up another tab."

"Urk! O-Okay…" Rei sniffled sadly as he took the money he'd just received and handed it to Lecia.

"One, two, three, four, five… Here's your change."

"Change? Why bother?! It's not even 500 piros…"

"I said you can run up another tab. You just have to pay what you owe when you have the money. Any objections?"

"No, ma'am…"

"Good."

Lecia left the sad Rei behind and walked into the crowd. There, she found a particular young man. He was Guinness, Lecia's younger brother by blood.

Lecia plopped down in a seat next to him as he slowly sipped at his drink.

"Here," she said.

"Lecia… Huh? Where'd you get all that money?"

"I collected it from Rei. He built up a real monster of a tab."

"Wow… I'm more surprised that he paid it off."

"This ought to be enough, right?"

"Huh?"

"Your marriage with Kiki. You can afford it now, right?"

"W-Well, yeah, but…"

"Don't make a woman wait, and don't be modest with your siblings. Go marry her and make her happy, young man."

"Y-Yeah…"

"Quit wasting time and go propose! I'll take the money for now, and I'll make sure it gets in the right hands when it's time to prepare for the wedding and stuff."

"B-But what if she says no?"

"The whole damn village is waiting for you two to get hitched. Just go!"

"O-Okay, fine!"

Chased off by Lecia, Guinness ran to find his hard-working childhood friend Kiki, who was at this time taking orders and dishing out food and drink.

And after that…

"M-Mr. Sato!"

While I drank with the chief and company, explaining the economic activities around dungeons as best I could, a man and a woman approached me.

One was a girl named Kiki who'd already come by a few times, while the other was a slender young man I hadn't met before.

"Hi there," I said to them. "Who are you, young man?"

"M-My name is Guinness. Excuse me, Mr. Sato?!"

"Yes?"

"Please be our marriage broker!"

"Marriage broker? Are you two getting married?"

Guinness nodded, and Kiki looked down, appearing rather shy—a surprising change from her previous liveliness. Still, she didn't look to be against it. In fact, she seemed so happy that one might think this was the most important moment in her life.

"Really? Well, congratulations," I said as I raised a glass to celebrate the occasion. Then, I suddenly remembered something and asked the chief, "Is it right for me to be their broker, though? It's not bad for the village in any way, or whatever?"

"Don't be silly. It is an honor to have our savior be their marriage broker. That's why Guinness asked you."

"Huh. By the way, I'm single myself. Is that an issue?"

"Not at all. There's no reason that you should have to be married yourself."

"All right," I assented, poured alcohol into two untouched cups, then handed them to Guinness and Kiki. "I'll do it. Congratulations, you two."

"Thank you so much!"

"Thank you."

We raised a toast. They held hands and flushed deeply, either due to the alcohol or the joy—or both.

With that, I turned to Alice and said, "That's what I mean."

"Huh?"

It seemed she still didn't know.

Stagnant villages like this tend to really jump into action when you throw large amounts of money into them.

That was how it had been during my overseas trip. The millions of yen invested by my Japanese corporation had served as the impetus for their stagnant economy to begin moving at incredible speed.

One destination for all this money would be weddings.

Guinness and Kiki's joy... I didn't know how the million piros had moved through the village, but I was certain that it was what had led to this.

But most of all, I knew that a simple million piros would make its way through this community and bring much greater wealth than that number could express.

94.

Two Bullet Hells

I revisited B2 of Aurum.

A hail of light bullets flew at me from the far end of a long, thin path. Alice and I took shelter behind a wall next to the path's entrance. The orbs of light missed us, slammed into the wall, and caused a burst of small explosions.

"So the path to B3 is up ahead?" I asked.

"Yep, I'm certain! It'll be right in front of us as soon as we get through here," Alice confirmed, with her monster friends sitting on her shoulders as usual. She looked sullen, her brow furrowed at the bullet hail that started the moment we were seen. "We can't avoid this, can we?"

"I won't call it impossible, but it'll be tough. Charging through ought to be faster."

"Charging through?"

"Yeah. Watch this."

I equipped my slime's tear, entered the hallway, and exposed myself to the bullet storm. Light rained upon me. The repeated strikes felt like I was being hosed head-on, making it difficult to push forward. However, I did not force myself to press on. Instead, I regularly healed myself with recovery rounds as I waited out the storm.

After a minute of being pelted, I felt something fall into my pouch. The pouch that automatically gathered drops had collected gold dust.

It wasn't much at first, but over time, it filled up.

Along with that, the storm began to weaken. I could walk where I couldn't before, and soon enough, I could even run through it.

By the time I'd reached the end of the hallway, the bullet storm had finished, and the monsters had vanished. In their place, my pouch felt quite a bit heavier than before. I held it in my hands to feel its weight.

Seems like 150,000 piros for going through a 160-foot hallway. Nice.

Incidentally, I'd used two recovery rounds. Walking forward while healing myself twice was all it took to make 150,000 piros.

B2 might be made just for me.

"Wowww! So that's what you're supposed to do here?" Alice asked.

"Only if you've got S-rank HP and vitality, *and* a slime's tear equipped."

"Sooo…only you can do it."

"It might work for you, too, Alice. Just gotta recruit a high-guts slime."

"The ones that can't die in one hit? I don't think I'd be able to make friends with one of them…"

"Are you able to tell whether they'll join you or not?"

"It's just a feeling," Alice said, though she sounded pretty confident to me.

Alice's "feelings" in dungeons couldn't be underestimated. Her intuition could discern the path to the next staircase, and she could tell whether monsters were around with over 90% accuracy. Maybe whether or not she could recruit monsters was the same.

We continued to follow Alice's intuition until we saw the path leading down to B3.

"I'll go first," I said.

"Wait a second. When you went to B2 first before, the floor I was on didn't change shape."

"Wow, really?"

I put a hand to my chin in thought. In other words, the entire dungeon wasn't changing shape when people went in; it seemed more accurate to say that a floor changed shape whenever someone stepped foot on it.

We'd only thought it was when people went into dungeons because people were going from the outside into B1.

"So what if we used Boney and Bubbly here?" Alice suggested.

"...Oooh!" I snapped in realization. "Like how you used them to help the villagers before?"

"Yeah!"

"You're pretty smart."

"Hehehe... Anyway, let's do it."

"Yeah."

I went down to B3 first. The moment I stepped in, my surroundings distorted and I could no longer see the way I'd come from.

I waited there. Before long, everything changed again.

It was my first time here, so I took off the pouch and waited as things changed over and over.

Alice was repeatedly sending her monster buddies down to this floor. After one came in and the floor changed structure, she'd return that monster to chibi size and call it back. She did this to change the floor's structure.

After a few dozen tries, I saw a staircase leading up to Alice.

"Thanks for waiting," she said.

"Good job."

Alice proudly stepped down to B3. Everything changed again, and we were both warped to a different place.

Monsters appeared.

"Whoa! That's a whole ton of baddies!"

"Another monster house, huh?"

We were taken to a gymnasium-like chamber. Little demons just like the ones on B1 and B2 mobbed us. One of them swung its hand down, throwing an orb at me. Unlike the bright ones of B2, though, it was surprisingly dark.

They were a black that didn't reflect any light, kind of like what I'd seen on the internet this one time.

"More long-ranged attacks, huh? Lucky us," I mused. "Alice, hide behind me."

"Okay!"

I confirmed that my slime's tear was equipped and took the black ball attack to protect Alice.

"Gah!"

Suddenly, an impact pierced through my brain. It was enough to make everything go white for a moment. I couldn't tell what had happened.

"Ryota!"

"Ack!"

"Ryota, are you okay?!"

"I'm fine!" I exclaimed, but then realized that the corner of my mouth was wet. I rubbed it with the back of my hand and found fresh, red blood. "Damage... That's a lot, too."

"Really?"

"Yeah... I haven't taken this much damage in a long time. Maybe not since that dungeon master...? No, that can't be."

I looked around; the monster house was teeming with little demons. There were at least fifty of them.

The monsters had slightly different firepower, but they were about equal. Did that mean that every single one of them had more power than a dungeon master?

"That can't be…" I repeated those words again.

This time, three dark orbs flew at me. I evaded two while protecting Alice, but I allowed the third to hit me.

Argh!

Another impact shot through my brain. I'd gritted my teeth in preparation for the blow, so I regained my senses fast.

"Ryota!"

"I'm fine…" I said as I fired a recovery round into myself to restore my stamina. "There's no doubt. These things are stronger than that dungeon master."

"Whoa… Huh? They're not?" Alice said, confused.

"They're not? What do you mean?" I asked Alice and noticed that she was conversing with her two chibi-sized monster buddies.

"Are they magic attacks?" she asked them.

"Explain, please!"

"Umm, they say that physical attacks are affected by vitality, while magic attacks are affected by willpower."

"…Oh, that's it!"

It all made sense now. I'd ignored it to this point, but it seemed like vitality was related to physical defense, while willpower was related to magical defense. My vitality was S-rank, but my willpower was still at F. In other words…I was basically at my original level 1 state on this floor, wearing paper armor.

This is bad. Really *bad.*

"So we're in trouble, right?" she asked me.

"Yeah. We'd better leave—"

Before I could finish my sentence, dark orbs flew toward me from all directions. It was an omnidirectional storm, just like last floor's.

If all of these hit me…I'll die, even with S-rank HP!

I gritted my teeth, put an arm around Alice's waist, and pulled her close.

"Hyahn!"

Then…I dodged. I weaved through the magical dark orbs. Each one I evaded hit the wall and created a small explosion, just as big as those of the light orbs. They were the same strength, too; the only difference was the one between my S-rank vitality and F-rank willpower.

If they hit me, it would hurt. I could even die.

However…I still had S-rank speed.

"Ryota!"

"Hold on tight!" I roared as I held Alice under one arm and made my way through the bullet hell, weaving through the dense torrent of orbs with as much speed as I could muster.

"Wow…"

Alice was astounded as I dodged each orb by a hair's breadth. Of course, I wasn't just evading; whenever I found an opening, I would counterattack with one gun.

With my concentration heightened through my evasive maneuvers, I fired off headshot after headshot at the attacking little demons. Their heads blew off, and they disappeared and dropped gold dust.

Eventually, my focus rose to its maximum. I was in the zone. Everything I saw, everything I heard, and everything I felt were enemies. Monsters.

Dodge, fire.

Dodge, fire.

I repeated that sequence single-mindedly.

"Wow… It's like a dance."

In the midst of that bullet hell, I annihilated all the enemies

without taking any further damage. But once it was over, I was more fatigued than ever before—I was spent.

Due to that stress, we didn't make much. We closed the day at only 300,000 piros, just a third of the prior day's earnings.

95.

To Go Even Further Beyond

Today, I decided to explore B3 of Aurum alone.

I proceeded down the narrow, twisting paths until an open chamber came into view. Despite being an underground dungeon, it had these spaces as big as gymnasiums. The inside teemed with little demons.

I loaded normal rounds and set my sights on my goal. But instead of going into the monster house, I stayed in the tunnel. This reduced my visibility, but it also made it so they had to enter a set area to see me, forcing them into my line of fire.

One shot, one kill...

I aimed carefully, firing off headshots one after another. When struck, the little demons fell to the ground and disappeared, dropping gold dust that was sucked into my pouch.

Little demons crowded into the tunnel and fired dark orbs. I fired back, undaunted.

Some of them shot dark orbs like machine guns, but I evaded them and countered with regular bullets.

It was like a gunfight in a movie.

I'd be in bad shape if they hit me due to my F-rank willpower, so I prioritized evasion in this fight.

Evade, fire.

Fire, evade.

After repeating this for a while, I'd mopped up all of the little demons.

I pinched the bottom of my heavy pouch and estimated the weight.

"Fifty-seven in total. About 200,000 piros?"

That was the approximate worth of one monster house. I'd made 200,000 piros from that alone, but I wasn't after money today.

I went into the open gymnasium, put my guns away, and waited a while.

After three minutes, another little demon appeared. As usual, it looked like the dungeon itself had given birth to it.

It didn't approach me, however. Instead, it fired dark orbs from afar. This monster fought from long range, after all.

I evaded the orbs with ease. It fired another, but once again, it was an easy dodge. It was just one, and they weren't very fast, so it wasn't all that difficult.

I kept on evading without countering until another little demon appeared. This time, it popped out of the ceiling like eggs out of an animal.

It fired dark orbs as well. I had two enemies on my hands now.

I continued dodging double the orbs, never counterattacking. This was still just playtime to me.

While I kept running around, a third, fourth, and fifth appeared. Little demons continued to be born, increasing the number of orbs being shot at me.

Of course, I kept going and collecting enemies without counterattacking.

Little demons continued to accumulate until it became a real bullet hell, heightening my concentration over time.

☆

In a corner of the village was the Swallow's Returned Favor's planned lot for an Indole branch.

They'd gotten right to work building their new office, but until its completion, they had to operate out of a tent.

Inside the tent, Ina treated my wounds. There was another female employee in the tent who sat at the counter and ran the shop.

"It threw me for a loop to see you injured when you came to sell your gold dust," Ina said. "I mean, I've never seen you like that before."

"Really? I bet you saw me like that a few times when I first started out. Back when I only had bean sprouts…"

In the earliest days, back when I'd farmed 20,000 piros to rent a room for Emily, I remembered being tattered and beaten every single time I brought back more bean sprouts to sell.

I didn't have guns back then. Likewise, I was out of recovery rounds this time, which was why I'd come back so beaten up.

"So, is Aurum really that dangerous of a place? It must be, if it beat you up so badly."

"B1 isn't that bad; you can solo it without too much difficulty. B2 and B3, you'd better have a party. You end up fighting a lot of enemies at once."

"Really?"

"Yeah. If you went alone…"

I had Ina pause her treatment, picked up a pebble at my feet, and tossed it up ahead. Then, I whipped out my guns!

Bang bang bang bang bang bang! I fired twelve bullets total from my two guns in random directions.

Then, I reloaded quickly and fired twelve more. After that, I once again reloaded and fired twelve more.

Reloaded yet again, fired twelve more.

In total, forty-eight shots. That was the number of little demons I'd evaded without getting hurt.

All of the shots I'd fired were homing rounds. Every randomly fired shot changed their arc and went toward the pebble.

Stardust: the technique I'd come up with when I defeated Nihonium's dungeon master, in which a whole bunch of homing rounds pierced through the enemy like shooting stars.

Forty-eight bullets struck the pebble one after another, shattering it. Eventually, it was gone without a trace.

"They shower you with cannon fire just like that," I explained. "So yeah, you really need a party."

"…" Ina fell silent.

"Ina?"

"Oh, umm, sorry. Do they do this on B2 and B3?"

"Yeah."

"And you went farming there?"

"Everything I brought you today is from B3," I confirmed. "How much did it come out to, again?"

"Just under 500,000 piros."

"Pretty big haul."

"Okay, but what did you do to deal with their attacks?" she urged.

I pointed to the spot Ina was just treating and joked, "I dodged them. Though sometimes there are too many to dodge, which is what made me end up like this."

"Y-You dodged them?"

"Not perfectly, mind you. I could do forty-eight just fine, but any more, and I'm in for a world of hurt."

"That's already awesome. I mean, it sounds crazy to be able to dodge that many."

"Awesome or not, it doesn't matter for dungeoneering unless you can do it consistently…"

I'd practiced evading them so that, even when I had S-rank willpower, I'd be prepared when it came to fighting stronger monsters.

Despite my S-rank vitality, dungeon masters still dealt a ton of damage with physical attacks. It was likely that there would be monsters out there that could overcome S-rank willpower, so instead of being lazy, I had to learn how to dodge things.

"I'll be taking a break from that training, though," I added. "All of my recovery rounds—healing items, that is—are gone."

"I see," Ina said, stood up, went to where the pebble was, and looked down at its shattered remains. "If only there was a place where you could do the same training without the risk of injury."

"Huh?" I gasped.

"Huh?"

"…Oh."

"Oh?" Ina looked confused.

I approached, took her hands, and gazed right into her eyes.

"Thank you, Ina! There *is* a place like that!"

"H-Huh?"

"Thank you! Thank you so much!"

After telling her I'd be back and saying goodbye, I sprinted off toward Aurum.

Left behind, Ina vacantly watched as Ryota ran off. Eventually, though, the look on her face changed.

"…Ugh. Men."

As she gazed at him, she closed one fist and put her other hand on it. Like a nun in prayer, she held her hands close to her heart.

"He's like a little kid when he talks about dungeons."

"You're one to talk. You look like a maiden in love," Ina's coworker at the counter joked, causing her face to turn red.

"Shut up! Why do you care?"

This was her just desserts for her doing the same to Erza once.

On B2 of Aurum, I danced amid a hail of light orbs inside a monster house.

Their flight paths and density were the same as the ones on B3; all that differed was that these were physical attacks, which meant that they had almost no effect on me with my S-rank vitality.

I dodged them, though, rather than taking the hits.

45, 46, 47, 48... I counted mentally. When not killed, the monsters accumulated over time.

Eventually, they went past the threshold at which I could no longer evade them all. An orb of light hit me. I was left unhurt, however, so I took a deep breath, refocused myself, and began evading again.

Ina had jolted my memory, making me remember the existence of a place with the same bullet storms yet no danger. I hadn't thought of training here because the idea that "I can take physical attacks anyway" had kept the idea of dodging these from ever occurring to me.

Now that I'd been made aware of it, I'd found the perfect training spot.

It was safe to get hit because I took almost no damage, but I evaded with the same mindset as on B3: if I got hit, I'd be in big trouble.

This training continued until nightfall, and I learned to dodge the bullet rain of up to sixty little demons at once.

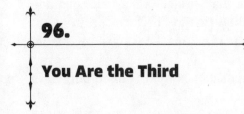

96.

You Are the Third

This brings us to B4 of Aurum.

After I waited for Alice to join me, she slowly said, "This is the last one."

"Is it really?"

"Yeah. There's no path down."

"Four floors in total, huh? It's pretty shallow."

Many of Cyclo's dungeons went beyond ten floors. The one that had formed called Selenium after I came to this world was ten floors, too. Compared to them, four wasn't much.

"So, what are the monsters here like?" I asked, checking my ammo and preparing for battle. Suddenly, Alice looked off into a random direction and noticed something. "What's the matter?"

"Eve's really strong, right?" she murmured.

Eve was currently on B2. She'd claimed that she was bored, so she came into this dungeon, but we ended up leaving her there.

"Yeah. She broke those orbs of light with her chops. It's no wonder she became famous sooner than me. I hear she used to go into really deep floors with her old party all the time."

"Wow. What happened to their party?"

"Eve said they had 'fundamental differences in dungeon priorities.'"

Alice cocked her head and asked, "Dungeon priorities?"

Don't ask me. I don't even know the answer myself.

"Based on how she phrased it, I'd guess it's like when bands have 'musical differences,' but I don't know any details."

"Huh... Wow, I wish I was that strong," Alice said, sounding kind of sad. Boney and Bubbly tried to cheer her up from her shoulders. "Thanks. And you're right, maybe we just need more buddies."

She looked sad at first, but she was right back to normal in no time.

Alice had already reached her level cap of 2, and her stats were painfully average. She would need more buddy monsters if she wanted to get stronger.

Skeleton Boney and slime Bubbly were already by her side, but there were only two of them, and they weren't very strong. Even when they visited dungeons with her, she couldn't offer much help in a battle.

We walked around for a while until we ran into a monster. Just like on the previous floors, it was a slightly recolored little demon. As soon as it saw us, it swung its arm down.

Its hand shone.

Is that a light orb?!

I prepared to evade it, but *poof*, the light in its hand disappeared.

"Nothing happened. What's going on?" Alice asked.

"I dunno."

The little demon swung its arm again. This time, its hand turned black. In fact, it was so black that it looked as though there was nothing there, only sucking in light.

Is it going to use a magical dark orb?!

I tensed up, but it once again made an airy *poof* that resulted in nothing.

"Nothing happened," I noted.

"It's flustered! It's kinda cute."

I had to agree with Alice. It was a monster, but it looked at its own hands and swung them around frantically. It looked like a kid panicking, which was just adorable.

"What should we do with it?" I asked Alice.

"I dunno. What do you think?"

"I'd...feel a little bad killing it."

"Do we let it go?"

"Maybe..."

I held my chin in thought. Just then, the little demon started acting differently. Its eyes began to spin from its futile efforts, and steam started blowing from its head. In midair, it pretended to stamp on the ground. Right after that, it clenched its fists and thrust them upward.

After striking this fist-clenched banzai pose, light emitted from its body. And not just from its body—from *within* its body. It cracked, and light began to leak out.

"This is bad!"

I ran in front to protect Alice. A magic circle spread around the little demon's feet and then burst. The monster itself had burst!

A suicide bomber.

While I covered Alice, powerful explosive winds struck me. I gritted my teeth to withstand it.

In what felt like both an instant and forever, a torrent of light and sound swallowed me whole.

After some time, the light and sound faded. I breathed a sigh of relief. My body stung all over and my ears were ringing, but the damage itself wasn't that bad.

"Phew..."

"Ryota! Are you okay?!"

"I'm just fine. How about you, Alice?"

"You covered me, so I'm okay... Thank you."

"I'm just glad you're safe. So that was like a suicide explosion, right?"

"Yeah, it seemed like it."

"We'd better tighten our defenses."

"Okay!"

I protected Alice as we proceeded onward. Using her monster-sensing guidance, we approached the closest group of monsters.

This time, there were three. They all looked the same.

They swung down shining hands and misfired.

They swung down dark hands and misfired.

Then, they exploded.

Three explosions assailed us at once. As I covered Alice, I realized something: before they exploded, I'd witnessed only one of them pretending to stomp on the ground; the other two were in the black hand stage. And yet, the magic circle had made them explode, too.

So one of them served as the trigger for the other two to explode, I hypothesized.

"Owwies..." Alice groaned.

"Are you okay?"

"Yeah, it's not too bad. This floor is really rough, though. They don't even drop anything when they explode, right?"

"They sure don't."

"Do we have to beat them before they explode?" she suggested.

"Let's try it."

"Then let's go this way! There's one all alone here."

Alice guided me to a single little demon. It swung its arm, which emitted light, and misfired—but I fired a regular bullet that was powered up by buffing rounds.

We couldn't have it exploding on us, so I wanted to kill it in one hit.

It was a headshot, knocking the little demon's head clean off.

"So?" she urged.

I didn't have my pouch equipped, since this was a new floor, so I went to where the little demon had fallen and disappeared. There, I confirmed that gold dust had fallen to the floor.

"We have ourselves a drop," I announced.

We found another and let this one explode. This time, though, I used a full-powered freeze round to create a wall of ice that protected us.

This one dropped nothing.

"Seems like a no?" Alice said.

"Yeah, I have a good idea how this works now. The little demons on this floor follow a set action routine. They fail to use a light orb, fail to use a dark orb, stomp, create a magic circle, and explode."

"And then they blow up any friends alongside them."

"Yeah. It seems like any monsters inside the magic circle explode, and the power scales linearly per monster."

"What would happen in a monster house, you think?"

"Stop scaring me!" Just imagining it made me shudder. A whole crowd of little demons in that big, open space... I imagined the sight of just one of them finishing their misfires and creating a chain reaction.

"So this floor is special, too," Alice mused.

"Yeah, they're gonna need to create a permit for this one. Still, they don't drop anything if they explode. Once word of that gets around, the only adventurers coming here will be the ones confident that they can take them down fast."

"True..."

Ninety-nine percent of any person's reason to delve into dungeons was to collect drops. If they couldn't obtain this monster's drops, then there was no point in coming this way.

I figured they ought to limit it to adventurers with permits, though it would effectively be the same with or without.

"Oh!" Alice gasped.

"What's up?"

"Someone's calling me."

"Calling you? Hey, wait!"

Alice ran off. I scrambled after her.

Through the slim passages of the dungeon, we rounded multiple corners until we found a single little demon. It swung its arm down, which glowed white, and misfired.

"Wait, hold it! Listen to me!"

And yet, Alice tried to speak to it, for some reason.

The little demon swung once more. This was the second part of its routine, two parts before the explosion.

"Boney, Bubbly! Stop Boomy!"

The skeleton and slime turned to their normal monster size— normal size, yet still chibi appearance.

Alice and her buddies charged toward the little demon. It began to stomp—

This is bad!

I swiftly changed bullets to five buffing rounds and one restraining round. Then, I fired the full-powered restraining round at the little demon.

Light bound the demon, keeping it from stomping. The magic circle didn't appear.

"Thanks, Ryota!"

With the little demon restrained, Alice went to face it. All three of them attacked the little demon: Alice, Boney, and Bubbly. One was only level 2, and the others were first-floor monsters. It took them a full minute to defeat the restrained little demon.

After a while, the ropes of light disappeared, and the little demon fell to the floor. Before it disappeared, Alice cradled the monster in her arms.

It disappeared with a pop—and then became a new being. Like Boney and Bubbly, it became a palm-sized, chibified little demon. Its name was probably Boomy, given what she'd been saying earlier.

"Nice to meet you, Boomy!" Alice squinted happily at her new companion.

With their job done, Boney and Bubbly returned to their usual size and sat on her shoulders once more.

"I'm Alice! My friends here are Boney and Bubbly. We're so happy to have you!"

The monster buddies introduced themselves through Alice's speech and their own body language. The sight was kind of cute. But for some reason, Boney and Bubbly hid behind her back.

What's the matter? I wondered. However, the reason became clear soon enough.

"Huh? Will the explosions get you, too? It'll force you to explode if you're in the circle? Oh…"

This is funny and *terrifying.*

97.

Bomberdemon

We encountered a single exploding little demon on B4.

The moment we got there, Alice held her hand out and sent her new buddy into battle.

"Go, Boomy!"

It returned from plushie size to regular size, though our little demon continued to be in a cute chibi form despite being the same size as the enemy.

The opposing little demon swung its hand twice, misfiring both times as usual. It did the routine we were used to, but Alice's Boomy flew in a straight line and held its hands up in that banzai pose.

A magic circle spread under it, and light leaked from within Boomy. A second later, it blew up. That explosion was just as powerful as the original.

Once the explosive storm calmed, nothing remained there.

"Wow! Boomy, that was so cool!"

"So when it blows up, it doesn't die along with the enemy?" I muttered, gazing at Boomy.

It had returned to plushie size and gone back to Alice's shoulder and was now frolicking happily.

I'd expected as much given how carefree Alice looked, but it seemed Boomy didn't die when it exploded. When it turned into normal size and exploded, it just returned to small size.

"Can it explode like that as many times as it wants?" I asked.

"Yep, that's what Boomy says."

"No restrictions, or anything?"

"Boomy says not really. Oh, but I guess it can't use it more than once in a row, since it can't go back to normal size for a while after."

"I see."

That meant we wouldn't be able to set off explosions like mad.

"So, you said something about Boney and Bubbly getting caught in the explosion before. Is that how it works?"

"Is what how it works?"

"Remember when there were three of them, and one made the others explode with its magic circle?"

"Oooh, did it?" Alice giggled, finding that funny somehow.

Huh. Did she not see that?

Despite being mid-routine, the others had exploded due to being in the first one's magic circle. That was instantaneous, though; it was less than a hundredth of a second, in fact, so Alice hadn't seen it.

"But it sounds like you're right. Let's try it!" Alice suggested.

I agreed and followed her. Before long, we encountered another little demon.

"Oh, it's a little too fast. Boney and Bubbly, go stop that one from moving!"

Following her orders, Boney and Bubbly returned to their species' usual sizes and ran over to the enemy.

The little demon swung a hand down, but they stopped it. Boney grabbed its arm, while Bubbly used its flexibility to stick to the enemy's face. It almost looked like the little demon had a slime for a head now. It reminded me of a certain card game character.

Bubbly, the Slime Menace.

"Three, two, one… Go, Boomy!" she counted down and sent Boomy out again.

Boomy flew forth, banzai posed, and created a magic circle. Right after, there was a flash of light and explosive winds ruled the area.

"Eep!"

"Whoa!"

I'd expected this to an extent, so I grabbed Alice's hand just as she started to lose her balance from the thrice-as-strong explosion. Then, I yanked her back and hid her behind me.

The wind was ultimately just wind; it made my jacket and pants flap around, but it didn't deal any damage to me.

Finally, the storm calmed.

"Thanks, Ryota."

"No prob."

"Good job, everyone!" she congratulated her buddies.

Three monsters had appeared back on Alice's shoulder. They all danced happily. The three chibi-sized monsters were oddly adorable when they were happy.

Despite their fear from before, even Boney and Bubbly expressed joy with their body language.

"I see. So the explosion differs based on which monsters are in the magic circle," I mused.

"Huh? Really?"

"There were three different explosions just now." I put a hand to my chin and analyzed each of the three explosions I'd seen in that instant. "There's the usual one from Boomy. Bubbly's was like bluish-white light bursting; it's probably ice or water elemental, or something. Boney's was black… Rather than an explosion, it seemed more like it was sucking in and swallowing its surroundings. It was like a black hole, so maybe it's dark?"

It was *only* an instant, and everything was jumbled up, so I couldn't be certain, but I wasn't far off.

"Wow… That's awesome, Ryota. You saw all of that just now?" Alice said in wide-eyed surprise.

"Wanna try it again? We could just send in Boney or Bubbly this time, though it might still be hard to tell, since Boomy will be there, too."

"Good idea."

"Let's go slower this time to account for the cooldown."

"Okay!"

Alice and I walked on. We walked, stopping intermittently to give Boomy time to recover for the next explosion.

I glanced at Alice.

This ability is what's more incredible than anything.

While we walked slowly, we encountered nothing. When we meant to, we found one monster. The fact that she could intuit everything about a dungeon, avoid monsters when she didn't want to see them, and limit it to just one monster to make things easier… I found that really cool.

"Say, Alice. Do you think you'd be able to go all the way to the bottom of a dungeon without running into any monsters?"

"I can! Oh, but not if they're blocking a staircase."

"Well, that's fair."

If she wanted, she could travel through a dungeon for days on end without ever running into something. Plus, she could also beeline straight for a monster if she so desired.

Yeah, that's a stupid-strong ability.

"But Boomy's a little difficult," she complained. "If it explodes, it can't fight for a while."

"That firepower isn't bad, but when it comes to dungeon farming, you'd be stuck fighting, resting, and repeating over and over. Not very efficient, for sure."

"Yeah. Oh, but don't feel bad, Boomy! It's not your fault!" Alice consoled her sad buddy. Boney and Bubbly tried to cheer the little demon up, too. Even in a dungeon, that was such a calming sight.

It didn't take us long to find another monster. This one was a single exploding little demon, too.

Alice sent Boney out alone. The skeleton went to stop the little demon from doing its routine.

Next, she sent Boomy.

"Do the thing, Boomy!"

The chibified little demon nodded vigorously.

While I wondered what "the thing" was, Boomy flew past Boney and the enemy. Now on the opposite side of them, it struck the banzai pose.

A magic circle spread out, just barely encompassing Boney and Bubbly as well. Then, boom: three explosions. Alice and I got away from them to escape the violent winds.

In the midst of the powerful gust, I said to Alice, impressed, "Oh, I get it. That makes it easier to see the explosion."

"Yeah! I saw it too this time. Boney's was a black, round thing, kinda like your annihilation rounds! Just weaker."

"You're right, they are like my annihilation rounds...just weaker."

"Yep!"

After agreeing, Alice suddenly piped up, "Oh, Boomy, congratulations!"

"What's going on?" I asked.

"Boomy leveled up from that!"

"Wow, so monsters can level up, too?"

"Yep!"

The chibi-sized Boomy was dancing harder than before. The

way it waved its arms and jumped around was cute.

"What happens when they level up?" I asked her.

"Well…"

Before Alice could answer, Boomy stopped dancing, turned to me, and swung an arm down.

"Is it trying to…?"

"Yep! It can toss out orbs of light now!"

"Very cool."

After waving its hand, the chibi-sized Boomy put that same hand on its hip with a proud look on its face.

So when monsters level up, they gain new abilities.

"If it levels up more, do you think it'll be able to use the black ones, too?"

"Maybe! Let's do our best to find out, Boomy!"

Alice cheered on the monster standing in her hand. Boomy pumped a fist into the air.

Dark orbs, huh?

I recalled the second step of this enemy's routine: the arm-swing. It was the same motion as the second and third-floor monsters when they shot orbs at us.

I had a feeling Boomy would be able to do it.

"If it can do that, it should be able to both farm and fight strong enemies."

"Yeah!"

With her three buddies by her side, Alice flashed a big smile.

98.

An Unusual Drop

On B4 of Aurum, I crossed my arms and watched a battle unfold. Alice was fighting now—or more accurately, her buddy monsters were.

The skeleton Boney was using its femur as a stick to hit enemies, the slime Bubbly bounced around and tackled foes, and our new friend Boomy used orbs of light as backup fire instead of exploding.

They weren't all that strong, but they were able to gang up on a single little demon and defeat it three-to-one. It dropped a speck of gold dust, which Bubbly picked up in its mouth and brought to Alice.

She accepted it and hugged Bubbly tight.

"Good job, Bubbly! And you too, Boney and Boomy!"

"Looks like you can fight from a safe distance now."

"Yeah!"

"If you can fight here, then you'll do just fine in Cyclo. Oh? Wait, you know, high-guts slimes counter overkill damage, but I wonder what would happen if Boomy blew up next to one…"

"I dunno."

Alice cocked her head, seeming interested in the answer.

"How about we try it when we go home?"

"Okay!" she agreed, returned her three monsters to chibi

size, and gazed at the gold dust she'd produced.

That was our fifth grain of the day.

Unlike the gold dust from my old world, the monsters here dropped pure gold, making the price of it very high. The grain in her hand alone was worth 10,000 piros.

"This might be the first time I've ever made money…"

"Come to think of it, you were always playing the support role in Cyclo, right?"

"Yeah!" she exclaimed, then looked at her hand, me, and her hand again. "Thank you, Ryota! It's all because of you."

"How about you thank your buddies there, instead?"

"Good idea! Thanks, everyone!" Alice said with a full smile. Her friends expressed their joy, too. "Hey, Ryota? Is there anything you want?"

"Anything I want?"

"I want to use my first earnings on a present for you."

"…Let's not, okay?"

"Why?"

"It's gonna make me feel old and sad," I explained. I appreciated her feelings, but my brain saw this situation as a kid giving her father a present with her first paycheck. Again, I really appreciated the sentiment. It just made me sad. "Let it stay in your heart, okay?"

"In my heart…" Alice thought for a moment. Then, she slowly approached me, stood on her tiptoes, and kissed me on the cheek.

"Alice?"

"That's what's in my heart."

"Oh, well, er, that's not…"

"I love you, Ryota!"

"Okay, then." I grinned sheepishly. What was in her heart was pure, innocent gratitude. It felt nice to be on the receiving end of that.

"Is that a problem?"

"No, I'm glad you feel that way."

"Oh… Well, thank you!"

For some reason, she thanked me again.

The warmth left on my cheek, the faint scent… With that lingering joy, Alice and I returned to the surface.

Along the way, I decided to strike up a conversation by summarizing my thoughts on Aurum.

"So Aurum is four floors in total. All floors drop gold dust, so all of the rares probably drop gold chunks. It's a full-on mining dungeon."

"What's that mean?"

"As far as I can tell, different dungeons have their own drop patterns. Aurum seems to be more like Selenium than Tellurium in this regard: instead of being usable items, the rare monsters drop more of what the rest of the dungeon produces."

"I see."

"I'd say we can wrap up our investigation here," I decided. "We should head back to Cyclo soon."

"Okay! I miss Emily's meals and my bed, too. I've been a little sleep-deprived…"

"But this is your village, right? Isn't it your home, too?"

"Yeah, but Emily's something else."

"Gotta agree with you there."

Whether it was a three-story detached home, a new two-bedroom apartment, or a crappy 20,000-piro apartment, Emily's work had turned all three of our rentals into bright, warm, lovely homes.

I knew I would have trouble adjusting to Indole, but even former resident Alice was having trouble sleeping in her own house.

"Next time we go somewhere, we should bring Emily!"

"Agreed."

We chatted while we returned the way we came.

The thin dungeon path split into a Y-shape. Alice stood in front of it and compared the two paths.

"The right one has monsters," she said. "It's not a monster house, though; I think they're just normal ones. Left… I don't think anything's there."

"Then let's go right. Might as well make some money on the way back."

"Okay!" Alice agreed.

We moved to take the right path. But just as I took that first step, suddenly, I froze up.

"Ryota? What's wrong?"

"This way…" I mumbled.

"You mean left? But there's nothing there."

"…No, something's there."

"Huh?"

"I feel something here," I claimed. I gazed down the left fork of the tunnel, which curved and made it impossible to see further. For some reason that I didn't know, I sensed something there. "I'll go see if it's actually empty."

"Huh? Okay, I'll go with you."

"No, it's fine. You go right. Level up your buddies, especially Boomy. You'll be better off once it can shoot those dark orbs."

"Okay. See you later!"

"Yeah, later."

I split from Alice and took the left path. Just as she'd intuited due to her being born in a dungeon, there were no monsters this way. The tunnel was so peaceful, so devoid of monsters, that it was easy to forget I was in a dungeon.

"Was I just imagining it?"

I started to feel like the sensation from before was mistaken. And yet, I pressed on. If there was nothing there, then fine; I'd confirm that and go home.

Eventually, I got through the thin tunnel and arrived at a somewhat open chamber. It wasn't too big. Perhaps the size of a garage, able to fit a few cars.

There was nothing inside, however. It was a dead end.

"Guess it was nothing after all," I chuckled dryly to myself. I should've trusted Alice; she was the one who was born in a dungeon and could intuit anything about them, after all.

I turned around to leave, but…

"Ngh!"

Suddenly, pure instinct made me react. I jumped as hard as I could to the side, and something gouged a chunk out of the ground where I'd just stood.

I spun around in midair and landed, whipping out my guns in the process. But I saw nothing. It was just an empty dungeon.

"…No. Something's here."

Unlike when I'd arrived, I *definitely* felt something now. Not because of the traces of the enemy's attack, but purely because I sensed a hostile presence.

To kick things off, I emptied both revolvers' cylinders, loaded them full of homing rounds, and fired madly.

The bullets flew forward, but suddenly, they did a 180 and rushed right back at me! I leaned back to evade the twelve approaching homing rounds. A second later, I heard a monster's scream behind me.

"Graaaaaagh!"

I righted my posture and jumped away from it.

The twelve bullets seemed to float in one location. If the enemy was human, that would be about where its head was. Space around the bullets was distorted.

It was as if it was transparent, but not fully. It was a demon's head. This one had the same appearance as the first floor's rare monster, but it was transparent.

I knew something was here.

I got a little excited. After all, if my estimations were correct, this one would become a gold chunk worth a few million piros.

It couldn't go fully invisible anymore. Thanks to my homing rounds hitting it and staying lodged in its head, it was unable to conceal itself from my gaze.

It swung its hand down, but nothing happened—

No!

Remembering Boomy, and the little demons of this floor, I jumped to the side.

The ground where I'd stood exploded. It swung another hand down, and something invisible flew my way, gouging out the floor.

He had at least two invisible projectiles. And worse—

"You can explode, too?!"

I couldn't waste my time here; I had to finish this quick. The invisible demon swung its arm down again. I dodged sideways—

"Nrgh!"

There was a hefty impact to my belly, as if I'd been hit by a hammer.

I saw the demon's not-quite-invisible mouth curl into a grin. Its invisible projectile had hit not where I'd stood, but where I'd tried to dodge to.

You little… That actually hurt.

Both my blunder and its smug grin ticked me off.

I put my guns away. Then, I dropped my stance, planted my feet firmly into the ground, braced myself, and jumped with all my strength.

Using my S-rank speed to the fullest, I charged in.

I saw surprise on its face. At the same time, the demon swung one arm down. I stopped it before it could finish, startling it once more.

It swung its other arm, which I also caught. I couldn't see it well, but I knew I was clenching both of the invisible demon's wrists.

"You can't fire off any more now. It's my turn!" I shouted, front kicking it. I felt a solid hit, and the demon's not-quite-invisible head slumped forward. That kick must've bent it in two.

I kicked again and again, mercilessly pummeling away. When I kicked one last time, I pushed my foot in and pulled hard on its arms.

Creeeeeeak... Snap!

There was a snapping noise, and the transparent demon's face disappeared. My hands still held its arms, however, and the areas around its shoulders grew visible.

Its arms had snapped off from its shoulders. The demon's face, still not quite invisible, was dyed with shock and rage. Then, it tried to stomp on the ground—

"Not happening!"

I rushed forward and seized the demon's windpipe this time. Then, I pushed it into the wall, pulled out my gun, and shoved the barrel right into its mouth.

I pulled the trigger over and over, using up every last loaded bullet. They pierced through its throat and medulla oblongata, blowing its head half-off.

I let go, and there was a thud as it fell to the ground. Just to be safe, I pointed my gun at it and waited, but it did not move again.

Pop!

It disappeared with that familiar noise…and then came my drop.

That's another few million piros, I thought to myself. However, I was proven wrong. For some reason, it wasn't a gold chunk. Instead, a staircase leading down had appeared.

99.

Limitless

I gazed at the stairs and muttered, "I guess…I should head down?"

Instead of an item drop, a staircase had appeared after I'd defeated the monster. Moreover, this was on a floor that we'd judged had no staircase leading down.

A hidden staircase. A hidden *floor*.

My heart pounded with excitement, with anticipation for what I might find.

I checked my equipment: two guns, both with a normal, freezing, flame, homing, restraining, and buffing round within.

Normally, I would have loaded recovery rounds instead of buffing rounds to be ready for most situations. But due to our long stay in Indole, I was out of those.

Still, I knew I could handle most of what might come. Preparing myself to dodge instead of relying on recovery, I descended the stairs. The moment I reached the bottom, the staircase disappeared.

"So you have to clear some condition to leave, huh? Or else…"

Either way, the challenge wasn't over, so I decided to remain cautious.

I'd come to an unknown place. The higher floors had narrow tunnels, but this was a white, open space. It almost felt like a different world. Plus, the air felt different, too—same dungeon, different air.

I didn't know what might happen, so I tightened my grip on my guns and proceeded onward, remaining cautious all the while. Eventually, I reached a more open space. It wasn't as big as the gymnasiums from before; it was more like a park in a residential district.

One man was there. Or rather, a monster. Silver hair and a beard, wearing a black cloak—he looked like a noble with bat-like wings on his back and horns on his head.

The word demon came to mind. Unlike the little demons and half-naked, goat-headed rarer demons from above, this was more like a greater demon.

"Do you speak?" I asked, tossing the conversation ball into his court and waiting with my hands on my guns.

He slowly raised his hand, put two fingers together, and pointed them at me.

Shudder...

A cold chill ran up my back. I evaded sideways.

The place where I'd previously stood was gouged out without a sound.

"Not one to talk, huh?! That makes things a whole lot easier for me!"

I landed and fired two normal bullets as a preliminary test. Of course, they weren't totally normal; I fired them to fuse along the way. The piercing round, bolstered by a buffing round, flew toward its mark.

Pshing!

The piercing round stopped mid-flight and fell to the ground. On closer inspection, I realized that a magic circle emitting bluish-white light had blocked it like a wall.

"A barrier, or some kind of shield, huh? Well, how about

this?!"

I replaced the normal bullets with buffing rounds and fired a combo of a freeze round and flame round. They fused, creating an annihilation round. It struck the barrier, carving out an area of space and that portion of the barrier along with it.

The moment I fired, I charged forward, punched the half-destroyed barrier, and shattered it.

I closed in on the demon. I had one flame and one freeze round in each gun, so I could fire one more annihilation round. Thus, I tried to do so from point-blank range. However, before I could fire, he closed the distance between us. He was closer to me than even the barrels of my guns.

His red eyes left an afterglow behind him, now glaring at me from below.

Crap!

The demon swung his arm as if going for a body blow, but instead of balling up his fist, his fingers were outstretched, exposing his sharp nails.

I quickly struck him with my knee, deflecting his wrist with a kick and evading the blow. However, his nails, clad in a black aura, managed to graze my chin. They tore through my clothes, and something fell to the ground.

I jumped back, reloaded my ammo, and fired as I backed off. But he put a barrier between my flame and freeze rounds before they could combine. The fire and ice were deflected by the barrier.

"You learn fast!"

"..."

He closed in once more, wordless. Now that he'd figured out my fusion rounds, he had come for another close-quarters battle, so I fired my guns while fighting him off hand-to-hand.

Gun-fu: a close-quarters combat martial art using guns. I

used my own self-taught version of the style to fight the demon. His power and speed weren't too great; both were maybe A, or even B, at best. However, his magical barriers were strong, and his ability to learn and make snap judgments were astonishing. He memorized my attack pattern after I'd done it once, and when I evaded his attacks, he changed his own patterns.

This was a difficult foe. It felt more like I was fighting a human than a monster. In a way, he acted as he looked.

"Ngk! He's getting even sharper."

The demon's attacks continued to evolve. When he feinted and attacked from an unexpected angle, I felt sticky sweat on my back. My bullets didn't hit him, and a single homing round couldn't break through his barrier.

After a while, I ran out of flame rounds. My restraining rounds and homing rounds ran out without ever hitting him, too.

I was gradually being cornered.

"…"

It felt like he was smirking at me.

"It's way too early to gloat!"

Hearing a *snap*, I thrust my gun forward. Predicting that, the demon tried to slip in close to me again—but instead of firing, I swung the gun straight down and struck him with the grip.

Crack!

That was a different noise, one like glass breaking. The barrier shattered.

I aimed the barrel at his head and pulled the trigger repeatedly. From point-blank range, I fired every bullet I had—regular bullets in the right gun, freeze rounds in the left.

"How's that—Urk!"

He counterattacked. I dodged quickly as sharp nails flew my way.

I put some distance between us. Blue blood flowed from his

head. Not from the right side, though; the left side of his head emitted cold and leaked blood.

"What a coincidence. Magic works better against me, too," I bantered. For the first time, I saw clear emotion on his face: anger.

Despite shooting the same number of rounds, the freeze rounds had much more of an effect than the normal ones. Realizing that magic attacks worked on him, I tried firing only freeze rounds. However…

"Kh! Out of freeze rounds, too?!" I roared in frustration.

It had been a while since we'd left Cyclo, and I hadn't replenished my ammo.

I'd thought that I would be fine as long as I was just fighting Aurum's normal monsters, but the sudden appearance of this powerful enemy had proven me wrong.

Seeing that, the demon seemed to intuit my situation and smirked.

Still, even without special rounds, I had magic! And so, I used the first spell I'd learned from eating magic fruit.

"Tch! Wind Cutter!"

It struck the demon, but it dealt almost no damage. He took it without putting up a barrier. Unmoved, his grin remained.

"Damn…"

I backed off. He stepped forth.

I backed off more, and he closed in.

He was backing me into a wall again.

This is bad. I'm at a dead end here.

But just as I thought that, I spotted something behind the demon.

With that… If I can just get that… But can I? No, maybe I can. I have a chance. But it'll only last a moment… I have to turn the tides in an instant.

I backed off, getting away from it, running away from it. The demon chased me, closing in to corner me against the wall, that grin remaining on his face the whole time.

I was chased into the corner of the room. With a wickedly maniacal toothy smirk, he swung his nails at me.

"…!"

Now!

I raised my gun.

He smirked derisively at me like a human. His attack stopped. It was as if he was challenging me to use whatever bullets I had left. And so I obliged, firing…*behind* the demon.

"…!"

This was the first time he seemed actually shocked. But when he whipped around to look, he was even more surprised.

There was a little demon there, just for an instant. It was an outsider made from the gold dust that had fallen out of my clothes when I'd taken that first hit.

I'd shot the little demon with a normal bullet. The demon seemed confused as to why I'd done that.

Not that I'd explain it to him; my plan was to finish this in one blow, after all.

I retrieved the lightning round dropped by the outsider from my pouch, loaded it, and added five buffing rounds. I then shoved it into the demon's solar plexus.

"You'll regret looking down on me," I muttered as I pulled the trigger.

The point-blank shot hit him, and electricity enveloped the demon. Electric discharge crackled around him as he groaned.

Finally, he was charred black all over, and he fell to his knees before dying. Then, a single bullet dropped. It shone all the colors of the rainbow.

I picked it up, anticipation swelling. A drop from an enemy

this strong, possibly even stronger than some dungeon masters, had to be powerful.

The voice I heard was enough for me to tell just how incredible it was.

Please choose one limitless bullet.

I thought for a while, but I settled on the lightning rounds, since they had the biggest unit cost by far. The bullet shone brighter for a moment before changing appearance to look like a lightning round.

It was just a lightning round—but you knew it wasn't *just* a lightning round.

I loaded it into my gun and fired. Lightning struck the floor of the empty room.

I fired again. Lightning struck once more.

No matter how many times I fired, it never ran out. No actual ammo was consumed. I now had unlimited lightning rounds.

"Maybe limitless recovery rounds would've been the better choice," I mused.

That thought might've been proof of how I was growing to know this world. Safety always came first; if farming was my top priority, then maybe limitless recovery rounds were the way to go.

Not that lightning rounds were bad, of course.

Better get going.

Suddenly, I heard a voice.

"Congratulations!"

"Huh?!"

I whipped around in surprise. A girl I'd never seen before stood there. She was about 4'6", wore a gothic lolita sort of outfit, and had bat wings and horns like the demon from before.

"A monster?!" I exclaimed as I readied my guns.

"Nope! I'm no monster."

"Then…what are you?" I demanded, suspicious.

Based on her response, she didn't seem to be a monster. But why was she here? And why did she look like the monster from before? Many questions came to mind, but her next few words answered the majority of them.

"My name is Aurum. I am Aurum!"

100.

My Unique Skill Makes Dungeons Grow Even at Level 1

The girl in front of me introduced herself, sounding equal parts arrogant and amiable.

"Aurum... Your name is the same as the dungeon's?"

"Not just the same. This place *is* me."

"Are you...the spirit of the dungeon, then?"

"That describes it, yes," Aurum replied with a grin. Her beauty and mysterious aura were enough to make me believe her claim with ease. "Though by human standards, you might consider this form a monster! Wanna beat me up? If you win, you'll get a huuuge chunk of gold!"

If she was a monster, sure. But I could never kill someone this cute and, most importantly, someone able to communicate with me on a normal level.

"I'll pass," I answered and shrugged.

"'Kay. So, what's your name?"

"Ryota Sato."

"Ryota? Sato? Weird name."

That would be because this world doesn't have names like mine.

Aurum then said, "How many hundreds of years has it been, though, since someone last came here? Conquering the whole dungeon *and* defeating the monster on the last floor only presents a 0.000000001% chance of opening this door. Guess I can't blame 'em."

"Hundreds of years? Didn't Aurum just form?" I asked.

"Huh? You really don't know a thing, do you?" Aurum's eyes opened wide. "We're always here, becoming dungeons, *not* becoming dungeons, even moving around sometimes."

"Really? Also, 'we'?"

"Yep," Aurum replied sincerely.

Aurum, Tellurium, Nihonium.

We.

"Are there 118 of you in total?" I hypothesized.

"Uhhh, sounds to me like you do know about us."

"I don't, I just remember my HHeLiBeBCNOF."

"Your what?"

"You wouldn't get it, sorry."

"Mmm, well, okay. I only meet people every three hundred years or so, so if you're not busy, how about we chat for a bit? Not for free, of course; how about I give you this?"

Aurum raised a hand. She snapped her fingers, which were extending from the end of one lacy bell sleeve, prompting a mountain of gold to appear in the room. Literally, a mountain of it.

Gold chunks were piled up like cardboard boxes in a storehouse.

The gold reflected the light around us. It was dazzling, and in more ways than one—that pile could be valued in the trillions.

Everybody loves money. Usually, the more, the better. But this...put me off a bit.

"Keep it," I declined.

"What? Is it not enough? Fine—"

"More importantly, are you okay?" I urged.

"...Huh?"

My question took Aurum by surprise. She froze up, eyes wide.

"Me? Okay?"

"Yeah."

"What's 'okay'? I mean, of course I'm okay. Look at me," Aurum declared with her usual arrogance. But at the same time, that sociability from before was still there.

This made me even more certain. What I saw, *felt*, in her wasn't just my imagination.

Emily. Celeste. Alice. Margaret. The people of Indole. All of their faces and all of their auras ran through my mind like a kaleidoscope. All of them were just like how I used to be—just like the corporate slaves of my world. It was the aura given off by the unfortunate. People who *weren't* blessed by their circumstances, with things forced upon them instead of living as they please.

Aurum had that very aura. It's hard to perceive sometimes, but I knew it was there.

"Wh-What's with that look on your face?" she demanded.

"What is it that you desire?"

"H-Huh?"

I said nothing, waiting for her response.

Finally, she caved and said, "Ugh, guess my poker face isn't as good as I thought. Well, can you blame me? It's been three hundred years, so yeah, I get lonely."

Aurum heaved a sigh, plastered a weak grin on her face, and answered my question, "I want to see the outside."

"Outside?"

"Yep, outside the dungeon. It's long slipped away from my memories, but it seems like I've been in this dungeon ever since I was born."

"All the time?"

"Remember how I said this body is like a monster? Monsters

can't leave dungeons. Heck, I can't even leave this room."

"...Wow."

Now I knew exactly what she wanted. It was so normal, so easy to understand. She'd never been outside since the day she was born, so she wanted to leave just once.

It was rare to see such simple dreams.

"Well, not that it'll ever come true," she sighed. "Since you're here, why don't you stay a few days? Tell me about the outside world, and I'll give you all the gold you want, 'kay?"

Her arrogance was concealed this time, while her sociability came out in full force. At the same time, something else peeked out: resignation.

Since you're here, why don't you stay a few days?

That request was genuine. If she couldn't go outside to see others, then she hoped that I could bring the outside world to her by staying here. However, that was a product of her resignation.

I can't leave, so at least tell me about stuff.

It was sad to see, so I put my gun to her head and pulled the trigger.

"Wait, what are—?!"

The limitless lightning round, powered up by five buffing rounds, singed the gothic lolita girl's body black in just one shot. She fell, crackled with electricity, and popped into a gold chunk.

It was a cube-shaped chunk of gold, about three feet long on each side.

"This sure is a hell of a lot of gold," I said to myself as I cradled the former girl in my arms. She was even heavier than Emily's hammer. Despite my S-rank strength, I still found her a little heavy.

With her in my arms, I left the hidden room full of gold.

On B4 of Aurum, I traced back the way I came. But before leaving the floor, I turned around. The staircase leading down was still there; it didn't look like it would disappear yet.

Relieved, I made my way to the exit with the gold chunk.

B3, B2, B1—I made it outside without running into anyone. There were a few people in the village plaza, but I aimed for an opening and managed to get through without anyone spotting me. Then, I left the village and took the gold chunk to a mountain summit. I put it there, along with a speck of gold dust, and walked away.

I then waited, waited, and waited for it to happen.

Eventually, a girl appeared from the gold chunk. She was just like when we'd first met. Not only was she unwounded, but her gothic lolita dress didn't have a single blemish on it.

"…Huh?" her voice rushed out in surprise. Aurum looked around, confused as to what had happened. "Wh-Where am I?!"

"Outside the dungeon."

"Outside?"

"Yeah. The idea came to me when you said you were like a monster. I figured if I turned you into an outsider, I could bring you outside."

"I mean, that works, but that was a stupid move," she warned me.

"Huh?"

"I can come outside as an outsider, but that means I can't go back. I can only exist on that floor. If I tried to go back, I'd disappear on some floor along the way. And if I'm gone, there won't be any more drops."

"No worries there, either," I assured her.

"What?"

"Watch this," I said as I pointed at the ground by her feet. The speck of gold dust I'd left there with her had also turned into an outsider—an outsider little demon that resembled Boomy, to be exact.

"This is… Hyah!"

Deciding it'd be easier to show rather than tell, I shot the little demon. A single limitless lightning round burned it black in no time. Then, it dropped an item: not gold dust, but a lightning round.

"Huh? Wh-What's going on here?" Aurum asked.

"I can just turn you into a drop again and carry you back inside."

"I-I can go back?"

"Yeah."

Aurum's eyes went wide. She was stunned.

"Which means you can relax and enjoy the outside world," I added.

"The outside… Ah…"

It was then that the truth that she'd made it outside sunk in. Aurum turned around and viewed the sight before her. The vast landscape, the vast world, viewable from this mountaintop… It was empty because everything in this world dropped from dungeons, but that made it all the more beautiful.

"So this is…the outside…"

She was overcome with awe. The raw emotion visible in her profile was now lacking the dreariness that had once underpinned the resignation I'd seen in her. I was glad that I'd let this little bird out of her cage.

After a while, still gazing at the sights, she said, "Thank you. Thank you for bringing me outside."

"If you like it, then that makes it more than worth the effort."

"But this is the first and the last time, huh? Going back feels like such a waste…"

"Last time? Why do you say that?"

"I mean, it's a 0.000000001% chance for that door to open. It only happens once every several hundred years."

"Don't you worry about that. Everything drops 100% of the time for me, and I bet that applies to the monster that drops your door, too."

"…Whaaat?!" Aurum screamed hysterically. "H-How?"

"That's just my ability. You saw me get a drop from that outsider, didn't you?"

"Actually, yeah…"

"Yeah. So I can just bring you out again sometimes."

"…Okay!" Aurum exclaimed, smiling like the little girl she was and pulled me into a hug. "Thanks!"

Her softness and brightness, so unlike the hard and heavy gold chunk she was before, made my heart skip a beat.

After a while, I tried turning Aurum back into a gold chunk to take into the dungeon. However, after I hit her with a lightning round, she dropped a mass twice the size of the last one.

Outsiders had different drops from their base forms. In the majority of cases, they were better. Aurum herself was no exception, dropping twice the gold.

I tried taking her back to the dungeon…but she was too heavy.

She was already heavy before, and now, she was twice the weight. Even with S-rank strength, my muscles were quaking trying to carry her.

I was getting tired, so I decided to put her down and take a break.

Aurum, you're heavy…

I'd never say that to a girl, lest I suffer her wrath.

Still, I'd managed to bring a smile to a girl who could have been locked up for hundreds, even thousands of years, so this was a small price to pay.

Though, that made me wonder about the other dungeons.

"So there are 118 of them in total. That means 117 more, huh?" I mused.

All of the dungeons in this world had spirits just like Aurum. That included Cyclo's own Tellurium, Nihonium, Silicon, and Arsenic, too.

"Maybe I should go meet them all."

Just as I was starting to settle into a dungeon rut, I'd found a new goal.

"Oh, there you are!" a girl called out to me.

"Alice? What's up?"

Alice ran over from the village.

"Hey, Ryota—"

When she saw the gold chunk, she jumped from surprise.

"Wait, what's *that*?!"

"Just ignore this, please. It seemed like you were in a hurry looking for me. What's up?"

"Oh, yeah! Ryota, there's big stuff going on."

"But what is it?"

"The dungeon drops have doubled!"

"Huh?"

"Everyone's getting double the drops, but why?" she wondered. "It's so sudden that a lot of people are worried. Do you think it's gonna be okay?"

"The drops have doubled…"

A realization hit me. I looked down at the gold chunk that was Aurum at my feet.

Double the gold. Or Aurum, moved by the sight of the outside world.

"…Wonder which one it is," I mumbled.

"Huh?"

"Oh, sorry. Ignore that."

I didn't know which was the cause, but I decided to assume the latter was. That made me feel better for having done all this.

"Alice."

"Yeah?"

"It's okay that the drops have doubled. Let everyone know that they'll stay that way."

"Really?!"

"Yeah."

"Okay. Got it!"

Alice nodded and ran off to tell everyone. I watched as she departed then gazed at the doubled Aurum. Now I was even more excited to meet the ones from Tellurium and all the other dungeons.

101.

Unearned Income

The next day, at around noon, I stood in front of the dungeon Aurum. From afar, I watched the overjoyed faces of villagers and the smattering of adventurers exiting the dungeon.

"It came as a real shock to hear that the number of drops in that dungeon had increased," Clint said. He looked just as amazed as he claimed.

Clint had come running the moment he'd heard the news. Though he'd doubted it at first, he had to believe it when he heard the stories of villagers who'd gone into the dungeon and the Swallow's Returned Favor employees who bought their drops.

There was no room for doubt when the raw numbers came in. Numbers don't lie, after all.

"Has something like this ever happened before?" I asked.

"As far as I know, it hasn't."

"Have you…ever heard of any special drops appearing on the very bottom floor of a dungeon?"

I didn't know if he was aware of Aurum's existence, so I tried to be as vague as possible.

"The very bottom floor? You mean the disappearances?"

"Disappearances?"

"Yeah. They happen once every few years, seemingly in some random place. The time, place, and adventurers themselves are all over the place, but all accounts claim that someone disappeared after defeating a rare monster on the bottom floor."

"Wow... Disappearances, huh?"

"Some of them come back pretty fast, but most are never seen again... Wait a second, did you...?!" Clint gazed at me with yet greater astonishment.

"Yeah."

"Really? You're a lucky one, Sato."

Lucky.

Aurum had mentioned that, too. That staircase only had a 0.000000001% chance of appearing when the monster on the final floor was defeated. Thanks to that low chance, I was the first person to reach her in three hundred years.

I'd met with her one more time yesterday, too, by once again defeating the rare monster to create the staircase. Aurum was surprised that I'd managed to get through the 0.000000001% door a second time in one day, but I wasn't.

I was the only person in the world with S-rank drops. My drop rates were 100%, I got better-quality drops than anyone else, and I could even get special drops from things that dropped nothing. Even 0.000000001% could become 100% thanks to my S-ranks.

So I wasn't lucky. It was normal.

Clint gazed at the villagers, who were all excited and vigorous thanks to the doubled drops, and said emotionally, "Just goes to show, you never know where you might find unexpected fortune."

"Huh?"

"I only sent you here to help the people of Indole. Never did I imagine things would turn out like this."

"Sounds like you got lucky," I chuckled.

"Yeah. Lucky."

We watched the village folk together. Suddenly, Clint held something out to his side so it was in front of me. It was paper rolled up into a tube shape.

"What's this?"

"Another stroke of luck. The Methylene issue was settled yesterday."

I accepted the roll of paper and opened it. The complex words there seemed to be a contract, and there were two signatures at the bottom.

"Indole has cut all ties with Methylene," Clint explained. "If the news of the doubled drops got to them before we signed this, that would've been a hassle."

"I see. Yeah, that is lucky."

I rolled the paper back up and returned it to Clint.

We stood side by side and watched the villagers working with smiles toward a better future. Some of them were adventurers from elsewhere. Economic activity was starting to heat up around this dungeon. Indole was on track to become a gold mining village.

That was the moment I knew my job here was done.

I split up with Clint and went to the chief's house.

The chief brewed tea and welcomed me courteously.

"What brings you here, Savior?"

"I'm thinking it's about time for me to head home."

"Head home? B-But where is that?"

He began to panic a little.

"Cyclo. I realized I've been away from home for a pretty long while now."

"Th-Then why don't you make Indole your home? We were

just discussing building a mansion for our savior."

"A mansion..."

Why bother discussing that?

"C'mon, you don't have to do that."

"But Savior, our village considers you—"

As the chief tried desperately to make excuses, the door flew open.

Eve entered and declared, "This low level cannot be detained."

Natural bunny ears, sexy bunny suit...

She ran over to my side and looked down upon the sitting chief.

"D-Detained? What could you mean?"

"Dungeons await this low level. *Other* dungeons."

"Other dungeons..."

"One dungeon and a village's selfishness aren't enough to justify detaining the low level."

"Mgh..."

The chief glared at Eve and faltered. Her eyes were unusually sincere.

"I-I suppose you're right... We shouldn't force our savior to stay."

"I'm glad you understand."

Just as he started to back off, the chief suddenly shouted, "Then please, at least accept our feelings!"

"Feelings?" I asked.

"Our feelings of gratitude. Everyone in the village wants you to."

Feelings of gratitude, huh? I didn't do this because I wanted anyone's gratitude, but that doesn't mean I should outright refuse.

"Okay. I'll accept your feelings."

"Oooh, thank you! I'd better let everyone know right away. We must at least give you the first portion of it before you leave, Savior!"

The chief stood up and dashed outside. It was his own home, yet he left us alone in it.

What an impatient guy. And what is this about feelings of gratitude? And the "first portion" of it?

"This bunny knows," Eve said.

"Do you?"

She nodded.

"The bunny has keen ears."

Eve's bunny ears twitched slightly. It was kind of cute.

"You make yourself sound like the king with donkey ears!"

"One percent," she said out of nowhere.

"One percent?"

"They want to give you one percent of this village's tax revenue."

"Those are some heavy feelings!" I shouted without thinking. "I mean, how much is one percent, anyway?"

"This bunny does not know."

"Figures."

How much would it be? We thought about it together.

We later asked Ina about it, who paused her work of putting the finishing touches on the new shop and answered, "Tens of millions a year, I'd guess. Oh, but with the drops doubled, it might go over a hundred million."

I was astonished by the knowledge that I would be getting a hundred million piros of unearned income per year.

102.

Bank Accounts and
Health Bars

B1 of Nihonium was as devoid of people as ever. I mowed down skeletons with lightning rounds.

Whenever the bullets struck, lightning rained down from the ceiling of the limestone cavern, shattering the skeletal monsters into pieces with ease.

They were strong—probably my strongest special rounds yet when it came to raw power alone.

"I bet it's 'cause their unit cost is so high. Or rather, was."

Lightning rounds came from the outsiders created by the gold dust from Aurum's dungeon monsters. It was gold dust, so the unit cost was about 3,000 piros per bullet.

Compared to the normal bullets dropped from veggies and the homing rounds dropped from trash, that was super expensive.

I fired them madly without hesitation. Every time I spotted a skeleton, I'd kill it with a lightning round.

See skeleton, fire a bunch. Even if they didn't hit, I could overwhelm the enemy with numbers. Not once did I reload; I just fired and fired away.

By going further beyond B4 of Aurum, I'd defeated a monster in a room that normally did not appear, obtaining a limitless bullet. It allowed me to obtain an unlimited supply of any bullet I wanted. The result? Limitless lightning rounds.

I paid no mind to efficiency now, since I didn't need to.

After a lap around B1, I had a pouch full of HP seeds, which I took outside the dungeon. When I arrived at the usual empty spot, I poured the seeds all over the ground and walked away.

Before long, the seeds turned into skeleton outsiders. I used lightning rounds for them, too, killing them and turning them into freeze rounds. With that, I had replenished my supply after using them all up at Aurum. And at no cost to boot!

I had to replenish bullets by fighting outsiders. Before this, my options were to either sacrifice time to save money by fighting them hand-to-hand, or sacrifice money to save time by defeating them with bullets.

"Now I've got the best of both worlds."

I gazed at the gun I'd loaded my limitless lightning round into.

Thanks to it, I could optimize both the time it took and the cost to replenish ammo. Things were getting more and more convenient.

I recovered the freeze rounds and went down to B2 this time.

The monsters were zombies, almost exactly as strong as skeletons. I used limitless lightning rounds to fill my pouch with seeds, went outside, and converted them to flame rounds.

Same with B3: I obtained loads of recovery rounds from the mummies there.

I'd started early in the morning, and it wasn't even noon yet. It had only been two, maybe three, hours so far. I began to feel like I could do anything with these limitless lightning rounds.

"…Oh, yeah. Things can't be that easy."

B4 of Nihonium greeted me with mummies who dropped vitality seeds and restraining rounds.

They looked just like the B3 mummies, but there was one decisive difference between them: in order to get their drops, I had to finish them off with recovery rounds.

When I encountered a mummy, I fired a limitless lightning round. The mummy fell, and its flesh disappeared, but the bandages remained.

I fired a limitless lightning round at the bandages. Since it was infinite, I went ahead and pulled the trigger a few dozen more times.

Repeated lightning strikes dug into the ground, changing its shape. And yet, the bandages still remained, as fresh and unblemished as before.

I took out my other gun, loaded one of the recovery rounds I'd just gathered, and fired. The bandages, which had withstood a hundred lightning strikes with ease, disappeared in no time.

This monster couldn't be finished off without a specific attack.

"Next time, I'm getting limitless recovery rounds."

Now that I could refill most special rounds more easily thanks to the limitless lightning round, I'd found my next objective.

Around noon, once I'd finished farming bullets, I left Nihonium and returned to our three-story house that was insulated from magic storms.

We'd equipped our garage-like first floor with a magic cart drop transport function, which resulted in the Swallow's Returned Favor dispatching Erza to be our personal drop buyer. It was basically an SRF branch office.

In there, Erza and Emily were doing something together.

"I'm back," I announced.

"Yoda! Welcome home!"

"It's been a while, Ryota. I see you're back," Erza greeted me with a smile upon this reunion.

"Yeah."

I'd gotten back from Indole yesterday, but I'd left so early for Nihonium this morning that it was my first time seeing Erza since my return.

"Thank you so much for bringing this to our attention before anyone else, Ryota. The owner was overjoyed."

"You always help us out," I replied. "I just hope it brings in some cash."

"That's an understatement! It's an enormous business opportunity. The owner even said we'll be hiring more staff to send there."

"What about Ina?"

"Ina's area of expertise is plants, so they'd prefer to send someone who knows more about gold or ore in general."

"I see. Fair enough."

She worked for a shop in Cyclo, after all, so of course ore wasn't her specialty.

"So, what were you doing?"

"I was just recording Emily's sales into her passbook," Erza explained.

"Passbook?"

I hadn't heard that word before, except maybe for bank transaction passbooks from my old world.

I looked at Emily. Indeed, our resident shorty was holding what looked to be a passbook. She looked like an elementary schooler on her way home with a piggy bank.

Noticing my gaze, Emily explained the situation to me.

"Erza may be working with us now, but we can't have too much cash building up here. That's why we've set up a direct bank transfer."

"Direct bank transfers and passbooks, huh?"

It's just like my world. Her explanation leaves no room for me to imagine anything else. So there's a banking system here, too, huh?

"Yoda, Yoda!" Emily called out to me. Her eyes sparkled as she looked up.

"Yeah?"

"Look at this."

"At the passbook, you mean…? Oh! You've got over a million piros now, eh?"

"Yes! This morning's drops tipped the scales."

"That's awesome. I've never seen a savings account with this many digits."

"Really?"

"I've never seen anyone's passbook but my own, and my take-home pay never went over 120,000 per month. Not enough to save up much, you know? I always felt like I was close to death."

Remembering my past made me both sad and mad. Working free overtime for a crappy company every day, constantly being exploited, having my HP constantly in the red…

"Low HP, and I still couldn't use my Super Special Moves. So sad," I muttered.

Emily cocked her head, confused, and asked, "Why don't we make a passbook for you, too, Yoda?"

"Make?"

"I bet you could get ten—no, a hundred million in no time. Yours could be even bigger than mine!"

"…You're right."

I'd used money as soon as I'd gotten it to this point, but upon Emily's recommendation, I realized that maybe enjoying the taste of savings could be fun.

103.

Half the Usual

The next morning, in the living room of our three-floor home, I ate Emily's delicious breakfast and gazed at the passbook made for me.

Celeste peeked over and asked, "What are you looking at?"

"It's my passbook, Celeste. Erza made it for me yesterday."

"You didn't have one before? Wait, why does it only have twelve piros in it? Don't people normally deposit easier, rounder amounts like a thousand or ten thousand?"

That was true. When you make a bank account, you'd normally deposit a single bill for convenience unless you had a special reason. Sometimes, people would deposit just 1 yen (piros) for particular reasons, too. It was unusual to see weird amounts like mine. But I did it for a reason.

"This was my leftover balance back then," I explained.

"'Back then'?"

"It was the end of the month. I had 912 yen in my account, so I deposited 100 yen to withdraw a 1,000-yen note from the ATM. That was the last of my money. I had three days until my next paycheck, but having that much left was a luxury for me."

"Umm…one thousand…yen, for three days? You mean piros? Is that what you were living on?"

"Yeah."

Piros and yen were almost the same, after all.

"Does that count as luxury…?"

"I think it is," Emily cut in as she brought food from the kitchen. "That would be enough for me to survive a month on."

"You're like one of those extreme cheapskates."

As someone who'd roughed it in dungeons, that amount of money seemed like a luxury to her.

"Emily, would you cook lasagna in the dishwasher?"

"…Lasagna? Dishwasher?"

"Mmm, yeah, I bet you could."

A look of confusion appeared on her face. Same with Celeste's.

I looked at the passbook again.

Twelve piros. My final remaining funds back in my old world. Numbers that would have my HP bar flashing red.

Purposefully matching that amount was my way of marking my new start in this world.

"Today, I'm going to make as much money as I can," I announced.

"Getting an early start?" Emily asked.

"That's the plan."

"Okay! I'll make and bring lunch for you."

"It might not be a good day for it, though," Celeste said cryptically, gazing out the window.

"How so?"

"Today's the day of the binary suns."

"Binary suns?"

"Yep. Binary suns."

Celeste nodded to me and looked back out the window again.

What's going on? I wondered, stood up, opened the window, and looked outside. Cyclo was pretty lively most mornings, but this was excessive.

Is it just me, or is it busier than usual?

Stores that usually opened around noon were already open, and people were already drinking at the open-air bar three buildings down. I realized, *I think...I've seen this before.*

"It's a lot like when magic storms roll in, isn't it?" I mused. "People couldn't make money in dungeons, so they'd hang out and have fun in the city."

Celeste approached and pointed up to the sky.

"It's because of that."

I traced her line of sight upward and gasped...for there were two suns.

B1 of Tellurium had fewer adventurers than usual, and even fewer monsters. And yet, I pushed the magic cart around as always.

It was rare to run into monsters today.

"This is due to the binary suns." Celeste, who'd tagged along, explained. "A few times a year, two suns appear in the sky. As a result, monster numbers and drop rates go down."

"I can tell at a glance that there are fewer monsters. But drop rates, too?"

"Yep. Everyone's drop rates are reduced by about one rank."

Celeste used the nearby status board to show me.

—— 2/2 ——
Plants F (-1)
Animals F (-1)
Minerals F (-1)
Magic F (-1)
Special F (-1)

The stats displayed on screen showed that her drops had indeed gone down by one rank.

"Like this, see?"

"I see."

"With fewer monsters and lower drop rates, it's like double the efficiency loss," she added. "Most adventurers don't bother going into dungeons on days like today."

"So that's why the city was bustling like during magic storms."

I used the status board myself and checked my own drops.

> ——— 2/2 ———
> **Plants S (-1)**
> **Animals S (-1)**
> **Minerals S (-1)**
> **Magic S (-1)**
> **Special S (-1)**

When she saw the stats displayed, Celeste said, "That's our Ryota for you. It doesn't affect you at all."

"Still no good, though. My drop rates might be the same, but the lower number of monsters makes it a net loss."

"That is true. Without monsters to defeat, there's no point coming here…"

"If only they'd increased in number rather than gone down," I grumbled.

"That does happen when the binary moons show up. According to eastern shamans, the yang energy of the binary suns suppresses monsters in all ways, while the yin energy of the binary moons makes them more plentiful and increases drop rates."

That sounded logical enough.

What about these eastern shamans, though? I'd like to meet those guys.

"So there can be two moons, too?" I mumbled to myself. Imagining it made me chuckle, but at the same time, this was kind of a slap in the face.

I'd wanted to spend today farming hard and bolstering my balance, so this timing was awful.

At this point, I might as well do something else until the binary suns leave.

On days like today, people would spend lots of money, consume goods, and create trash. So then, it was the perfect day for replenishing my homing rounds.

"Still gonna do it?" she asked.

"Yeah. It's a handicap, but I'm gonna do what I can."

"Good luck, Ryota."

With Celeste cheering me on, I decided to farm the dungeon despite the reduced monsters.

"Darn, you sure love to run!"

Twenty minutes after I'd begun farming, I noticed one—no, *two* things that were unusual.

First off, the monsters were weaker. Tellurium's B1 slimes were already weak, but their movement speed and attack power were basically halved now. Even a kid could take them down.

The other thing: they were a lot quicker to flee. Perhaps because they'd been weakened so much, many of them ran away the moment they saw me.

Binary suns weren't just double handicapped. They were *triple* handicapped. Fewer monsters, fewer drops, and added inefficiency from monsters trying to run away.

Due to the triple handicap, other adventurers complained and began leaving the dungeon.

"Ugh, I give up!"

"I didn't sign up for a game of tag!"

"Even if you catch 'em, they don't drop anythin'! I hate this!"

But I stubbornly remained. Thoughts of the number 12 in the passbook kept me here.

I gripped my guns tight and did laps around the dungeon.

I knew B1 of Tellurium well, so I went straight to monster spawn points. One out of every three attempts failed due to the monsters not spawning, but I took down each monster that appeared to make up for it. I mowed them down with liberal use of limitless lightning rounds.

Fortunately, much like with our battle against the Bicorn, He Who Defiles Purity, my S-rank drops did not suffer, so it was only a double handicap for me.

"...Really not a lot of monsters here," I grumbled.

Sometimes, I'd finish a lap around the dungeon and no monsters had spawned yet. That never happened on a normal day.

I sent 32,109 piros' worth of bean sprouts—not even the full 40,000 worth—and decided to move from the empty B1 down to B2. There were even fewer adventurers here, and of course, not many monsters.

I farmed B2 as well, getting drops from sleep slimes before sending some 20,000 piros and change.

This was way less efficient than usual, yet I farmed on.

After emptying B2, I continued down to B3 and hunted the monsters there to extinction. Then, I went back to the some-what-recovered higher floors.

But my efficiency only grew worse over time, resulting in half the earnings I'd gotten earlier. When I'd get bean sprouts, for example, I'd only get 10,000 piros or so's worth before I was forced to move on.

And yet, I farmed on.

That evening, in the Swallow's Returned Favor branch office that was our first floor, Erza greeted me upon my return from a full day of dungeoneering.

"Welcome back, Ryota. Well done today."

"Binary suns are the worst," I complained. "I don't want to farm on a day like today ever again."

"Binary moons are difficult in their own ways, since the monsters end up a little stronger."

"Uh-huh…"

"But the earnings are good, so many people think it's okay to push themselves…which ends up leading to some dying in dungeons they know well."

"Figures."

I sighed, expelling all of the air in my lungs.

I'm beat… Just plain exhausted.

A sense of futility washed over me. It felt like I'd returned to the old days, back to when I had no magic cart and had to go back to town when I had too much to carry. Hell, with how much I was walking, it might've been worse than those times.

"Okay, here's the summary of your deposit," Erza said as she handed over my passbook with a smile.

My passbook. The one that only had 12 piros before.

I took a deep breath and opened it, ready to see the damage.

1,219,001 piros.

In the passbook was a number with more digits than I'd ever seen in a bank account.

"Whoooa…"

The futility that had ruled my body to this point turned into satisfaction in an instant.

104.

Using, But Not Losing

The next morning, when I left for my usual Nihonium trip, there was a hole right outside our front door. Eve's face poked out.

"Bwah! G-Geez, you scared me. What are you doing, Eve?"

"Normal bunnies dig holes. Everybody knows that."

"I sure didn't."

"Fun fact. Smart bunnies dig three holes."

"I doubt I'll ever get the chance to make use of that fun fact."

While I rebutted, Eve crawled out of her hole and began filling it back in.

Eve Callusleader. A girl with very rare natural bunny ears and a tail who always wore a bunny suit. She had both cuteness and sex appeal in high supply, but despite her appearance, she was a hell of a powerhouse and a strong adventurer. Combine that with her overall weirdness, and I never had the slightest idea what was on her mind.

And because I had no idea, I decided to ask the girl herself.

"What are you doing here?"

"Low level, potions," she said cryptically.

"Hm?"

"I'm out of potions."

"Oooh!"

She meant potions, as in, the special items that only I could make drop. They were amazing things that could temporarily raise your drop rates. I'd produced a lot of them and let my friends use them.

"So you used yours up already?" I asked.

"Yes."

"All right. Wait a minute."

I U-turned back into the house, went into my room, and searched for the items. There were a few different kinds of potions, but I looked for the ones that would be most effective in Cyclo: the ones that boosted plant drops.

"Oh… I'm fresh out."

"You don't have any?" Eve asked, having come to my room with me. Her tone of voice was almost the same as usual, but she did sound just a tiny bit sad.

"I didn't get to make any during my time at Indole. Wait here while I make some more."

"Okay."

Drop-boosting potions dropped from money itself, so I took the passbook and left, withdrew money, turned it into outsiders, received potions, and handed said potions to Eve.

There was no issue making the potions themselves. After all, I'd done it plenty of times by now.

"990,000 piros…" I sighed.

My bank account balance, which had sat pretty at 1,200,000 piros the day before, was brought down a digit by the unexpected expense. That hurt just a bit.

I left Eve and spent the morning in Nihonium, where I raised my neglected D-rank MP to C-rank. In the afternoon, I went to Tellurium as usual.

If I had less savings now, then I'd just have to earn more, so I did my best to earn money.

By the way, I made more potions after satisfying Eve. The potions were mostly there to help my friends make more money, but to Eve, they were a necessary prerequisite for getting her delicious carrots.

I knew that blissful look on her face as she gnawed away at a carrot. Even if it meant losing a whole digit of my savings, I could never refuse her that.

In making those potions, my savings went down fast. And when I ran out of money, I just had to make even more. And that brought me to B1 of Tellurium.

With the binary suns gone, the dungeons were back to normal. There, I braced myself and mowed down enemies.

I killed slimes on sight, piling up bean sprout drops. Just half a lap, and I'd filled my magic cart to the brim. I flipped the switch and sent the drops back home.

Why was I so efficient today? Well, two reasons.

First was, of course, that the binary suns had left and brought the number of monsters back to usual. But also, there were fewer adventurers than usual—just like with the magic storm and the dungeon master's appearance.

Did it apply to the whole world, or just this city? Either way, when going into dungeons wouldn't yield much money, adventurers would distract themselves by going into town and splurging like mad. And perhaps because it took a certain kind of person to become an adventurer, many of them ended up going to bars.

And what happens once the magic storm has ended, the dungeon master is defeated, or the binary suns disappear? Well, despite the dungeon's yield going back to normal, many adventurers were hungover or still sleeping from overdrinking. The next day, dungeons would be just as empty as the day before.

Some would even drink to dull the pain of their hangovers! That would only drag them into a negative feedback loop, but we could leave those alcoholics aside.

It was my first time being here the day after the appearance of the binary suns, but I managed to get serious and rampage through the dungeon while the other adventurers were absent.

Another half-lap around B1, and my magic cart was full again. I sent the drops back home once more.

Now I had two sets of 40,000 piros, making 80,000 total.

I went down to B2, where Eve gnawed on a carrot drop. It was pretty adorable how she looked like a small animal.

Like a squirrel, almost. Well, I guess rabbits are small animals, too.

"Oooh, hard at work, I see," I said in greeting.

"Low level… You can't have my carrots."

"I wasn't planning on taking them."

In fact…

A sleep slime appeared just in time, so I killed it with a limitless lightning round. Then, I took the S-rank Ryota Carrot it dropped and gave it to Eve.

"Wanna eat this, too?"

"Low level, I love you, you are perfect, you can do anything you want to me."

"Oh please," I chuckled.

Afterward, I did a lap around B2, which was just as devoid of adventurers. But due to Eve's massacring of sleep slimes, my magic cart only ended up getting full after two-thirds of a lap instead of just half.

I sent that home. 120,000 piros total now.

It would hurt Eve's yields if I went too hard here, though, so I went straight down to B3 after that. There, I defeated the C-word slimes, turned them into pumpkins, and sent them back one at a time.

As such, I farmed on without rest. I wanted to get my bank account balance into the seven-digit range again, so I grinded the dungeon with all I had.

"Thank you very much. I will see to it that we take direct withdrawals from this point on."

"Yeah, thanks."

Earlier that evening, I worked in Cyclo instead of Tellurium. On the way home, our realtor Antonio happened to catch me. He'd come to collect rent that I'd left unpaid during my trip to Indole.

Seeing that I had my passbook, he suggested they withdraw my rent automatically. I agreed to that. I knew it'd be more convenient, so I figured, why not?

"You could've come and collected it sooner, though. Emily and Celeste were home."

"Oh, no. I knew you were away on a request from the Dungeon Association. Besides, Mr. Sato, you have my full faith."

"Thanks."

"Now, if you need anything at all, please let me know."

"Will do."

Antonio bowed and left.

My mood was a little spoiled now. I'd wanted to take my passbook home and have Erza record my earnings, but since Antonio found me, I had to pay rent.

Well, whatever. Gotta pay rent to live.

I pushed the magic cart along the way home. When I got to the house, Erza was the only one on the first floor.

Emily and Celeste hadn't returned yet. Eve and Alice weren't around, either. Only Erza.

"Welcome home, Ryota," she greeted me.

"Hey there. Here you go," I said as I gave Erza my passbook.

She accepted it, opened it, and recorded my earnings from today.

"Hmm? That's a lot of withdrawals."

"I spent a lot today. Consumables for going into dungeons, rent, stuff like that."

"I see. But goodness, this is something else."

"Huh?"

"You used so much, and yet… See for yourself."

Erza smiled and handed me my passbook.

I couldn't believe my eyes for a moment.

2,006,100 piros!

I had about two million piros left. Despite using so much already, I had two million, putting me above this morning's starting point.

I'd felt bad because I'd expected my savings to have gone down, but my excitement shot back up, making me happy again.

105.

More Taxes, Less Taxes

While dungeon snow fell on B5 of Nihonium, I farmed red skeletons. These monsters were three times faster than normal skeletons, which lowered my accuracy. I could hit most other monsters almost 100% of the time, but my hit rate was 90% at best with these guys.

It was clear how much more often I was missing.

"Kh!"

And they weren't just faster. If I failed to kill them and took too long to finish the job, they sped up more.

When I missed the first shot, they'd become even more slippery, reducing the hit rate of subsequent shots to what felt like 70%. That meant one in every three shots would miss.

Still, 70% wasn't bad. And I was using limitless lightning rounds, so it didn't matter—

"No, no," I scolded myself. "You're getting too conceited."

I'd begun to think that I could just take them down with wild, random fire, but I righted my way of thinking.

Like how I'd thought I was invincible once my HP and vitality were S-rank, obtaining new powers with the words "S-rank" or "limitless" often resulted in me getting cocky. This would, in turn, lead to me acting on the force of habit alone.

That wasn't good, so I forced myself to focus. In my mind, I began to count. I began with the 90% estimation from before—nine shots out of ten.

A red skeleton burst out of a wall—a unique trait of this dungeon—and ambushed me. I calmly evaded its attack and fired a single bullet through it.

Now, we had ten shots out of eleven: 90.9%, or an increase of about 1%. I picked up the seed, raised my MP by 1, and searched for my next target.

This time, one ambushed me from the ceiling. I steadily aimed and took it down in one shot again. Eleven out of twelve, or 91.6%.

But when I tried to pick the seed up, another red skeleton attacked. I dodged once more and rushed to counterattack, but this time, I missed. My accuracy was down to ten of twelve, or 83.3%, just from that.

"Mgh…" I groaned and took a deep breath.

My hit percentage may have fallen sharply from that, but if I got flustered now, it would spiral lower and lower. I stopped in place, took deep breaths to calm myself, and focused more. I then killed everything that attacked, aiming until the last moment each time to take them down. Constantly calculating my accuracy, putting my all into raising it.

Oddly enough, focusing on the numbers had a clear improvement on my concentration. That wasn't all; my motivation was higher than usual, too.

Concentration, motivation—with those on top of my high stats, I cleaved a path of destruction through B5 of Nihonium.

By the time noon arrived, I'd raised my MP from C to B. My accuracy went over 98% in the process, as well.

☆

I left Nihonium and returned home first. Erza and Emily were in the first-floor garage, so they greeted me as I entered.

"Good work out there."

"Welcome home!"

They sat on opposite sides of a table, drinking black tea. Sandwiches and bite-sized sweets sat atop the table as well. Despite it being noon, this looked more like teatime than lunch.

"Ryota, would you like one?" Erza offered.

"I'll brew more tea!" Emily said and ran up to the second floor.

I stood next to Erza, stooped down a bit, and took a sandwich in hand. It was a strawberry jam sandwich with just the right amount of sweetness. The food reenergized me, shooing away my exhaustion.

"H-How is it?" she asked.

"Hmm? How's what?"

"The, umm… The sandwich."

"It tastes good. Hits the spot, since I'm already pretty tired from this morning's work."

"…Yay."

For some reason, Erza pumped a fist in front of her chest.

"Why did you just pump your fist?"

"Huh? Oh, that was…!" she stammered.

Emily answered for her, saying, "Erza made that sandwich."

Her smile was even brighter than usual as she came down the stairs with my tea in hand.

"Oh, so you didn't make that one, Emily?"

"Right. Erza and I made them together, but the one you just ate is 100% Erza-produced."

I picked up another strawberry jam sandwich and chowed down.

"Mmm, yeah, that's good. I'd just assumed it was yours,

since it tasted good, but it looks like Erza's a great chef, too."

"Th-Thank you," Erza mumbled, blushing as she looked down. "Umm...may I make food for you again?"

"Would you really? I'd appreciate it."

"I will! I'll make so much good food for you!" Erza exclaimed eagerly.

I was excited by her enthusiasm, wondering what she might make.

I drank Emily's black tea and snacked on another sandwich, replenishing my energy.

"Oh, yeah. Just in case, could you record my transactions so far?" I asked, handing Erza my passbook.

"Record them now?"

"Yeah. I'd like to do this afternoon's farming with proper numbers in mind."

This morning, I'd calculated my accuracy while I farmed. Seeing that number go up with each kill was satisfying. It felt like I was accomplishing something. This was reflected in my concentration, giving me the motivation to keep on raising it. As a result, I'd made every shot from that point on, resulting in a 98% hit rate.

I wanted to try doing something similar this afternoon, keeping numbers in mind to see what would happen if I gave myself little victories.

Until yesterday, I'd preferred building up to a big accomplishment. Recording it all at once and seeing the huge growth in number was really satisfying. However, the strategy also resulted in me slowing down toward the end.

By building up small victories, I hoped to maintain my concentration the whole time and make more money in the end.

"Understood. Wait just a moment, please."

Erza took my passbook and recorded the transactions.

"Thank you for waiting. Your balance is building up."

"Really? It didn't go down?"

"It went up by about 500,000 piros."

"Bwuh?"

For a moment, I wondered why. I shouldn't have made any money since last night. The only reason I'd come here to have my passbook updated was because I'd gone and reported to everyone I could remember having business with. Because of that, I figured some money might have been withdrawn this morning.

I expected it to go down, not up. How is that possible?

"You're not kidding," I said as I read it. "That's almost 500,000. And the name is…Indole?"

"That's the name of a city."

"Oooh… Taxes!" I realized.

Right, Indole had promised to give me a portion of their tax revenue. It seemed they'd already made good on that promise.

"Taxes?" Erza cocked her head.

I described the gist of what had happened in Indole.

"I see… So that's why they share taxes with you," she mused. "That is amazing, though. It's essentially passive income."

"Yeah, I guess you're right."

Passive income. I like the sound of that.

It was a reasonable reward for clearing Indole's dungeon *and* outright doubling their drops, but it was still true that I was getting paid without doing any labor. Even if I did nothing from this point on, Indole would send me money.

From winning the lottery and living off interest, to building apartments and renting them out, and even to buying tons of stock and living off of dividends… Everyone dreams of living on unearned income. My heart jumped for joy upon seeing that dream manifest as a real number in my bank account.

"Whoooa… You're making money even like this? That's

Yoda for you, all right!"

"I'll still go to dungeons, with or without this."

"That's even more incredible!"

"...Ah!"

Suddenly, Erza seemed to recall something and clapped her hands once.

"What's the matter?"

"You've received another deposit... Wow, this is something else..."

"What's that mean?"

"It's your refund," Erza explained. "You've sold over 30,000,000 piros' worth of goods this year, which reduces your taxes a little. It began applying yesterday, so they've refunded the difference."

"Reduces my taxes? They don't go up?"

I returned my passbook to Erza, and she quickly recorded the new deposit. The deposit itself wasn't too huge; it was just 20,000 piros.

"Yes, they go down," Erza answered. "Did they go up in your previous city, Ryota?"

"Not really 'city,' but...yeah, kinda."

Due to how progressive taxes worked, there were points where you lost money by making more. That was especially true when I was a student. They didn't tax you until you made 1,000,000 yen a year from your job, but if you crossed into the next bracket, they started taking taxes and you lost money as a result. And so, I'd carefully adjusted my hours to avoid making that much.

"In Cyclo, your taxes go down as you sell more items. That incentivizes adventurers to put their backs into dungeoneering."

"I see."

I could understand that sentiment, though I didn't know what the side effects of that system might be.

A line item of 20,000 piros was recorded in my passbook now. Alone, that was a small number. However, the refund I'd earned due to my tireless efforts filled me with a sense of accomplishment.

106.

Time for a Career Change

I spent another morning grinding on B5 of Nihonium, killing hordes of red skeletons.

As a result of me keeping my concentration at the max from the outset, I'd managed to maintain a 100% hit rate. That tired me out, but I felt satisfied, too.

By the way, my MP was up to A now.

With two accomplishments in perfect accuracy and boosted stats, I returned to Cyclo. The city was as bustling as ever today. No magic storm, no binary suns or moons. No dungeon master, either. Adventurers were earning money, and the city was profiting from the booming economy.

My legs carried me toward my house on their own, but I soon remembered something and stopped. Emily had said something before I left this morning.

"I'm going in for hammer maintenance today."

Weapon seller Smith had provided her the Emily Hammer, which was customized to suit her needs, for free. Like athletes, famous adventurers could be sponsored by people who provided them gear. The better they performed, the more that same gear would sell. They were basically advertisers.

As a result, Emily was putting in some real work lately. Her level was capped, and she was kicking butt in Cyclo's dungeons—especially Arsenic, which was full of nothing but rocks. Thanks to those exploits, almost 90% of the adventurers in Arsenic used Emily-model hammers now.

"They're like Air Jordans."

It reminded me of some famous basketball shoes from when I was in school.

Anyway, Emily was out for hammer maintenance today, so there wouldn't be any hot food waiting for me.

"Might as well eat out, I guess."

I marched around the city, picking out the best place to eat at. It was then that I found a place serving something akin to ramen.

Based on the smell, it was probably tonkotsu or iekei ramen. The smell of that delicious, greasy goodness was so nostalgic that it drew me to the restaurant.

Pow!

Before I could enter, someone bumped into me from the side.

"Hey, sorry—" I tried to apologize, but I recognized him. "Huh?"

"Urk... Ah... I'm sorry..."

It was the man that a certain old man had been slave-driving along with a woman who was currently not with him. The old man had brainwashed them with the same lies about dreams that corrupt corporations loved to tell.

The person here was one such sacrifice. He...looked even more haggard than the last time we'd met.

"My bad. I was just spacing out a little," he apologized.

"It's fine, really. But...are you okay?"

"..."

"Hey."

"...Huh? Sorry, I wasn't listening."

He looked distracted. You might think his mind was elsewhere, but that wasn't it. He was so exhausted that he was going to a bad place. I could tell by the look on his face.

"Bye…"

"Wait, wait!" I stopped him as he tried to leave. Seeing my past self in him, I knew I couldn't let him keep going like this.

In the ramen shop, the man wolfed down food shockingly fast. He'd had three large helpings of ramen already, and the side of fried rice he'd ordered was long gone.

"Seconds, please! Oh… I'm sorry, I…"

"It's cool. I told you it was my treat, so go for it. Excuse me! Seconds for him, please."

Thinking he'd be too modest to order more, I ordered extra for him.

I'd pulled him into the ramen shop and promised to treat him because he looked ready to collapse. He'd tried to refuse at first, but when he smelled the delicious scent of his food, he fell to temptation fast.

You sure can eat, huh? Geez, slow down a little.

By the way, I couldn't eat anything at the place. The flavoring didn't really suit my palate. Not to say that the flavor itself was bad. The place was full of people all enjoying their food, so the shop was doing something right.

So why me? I wondered. It didn't take long for me to realize why. It was probably Emily's fault—or rather, *thanks to* her. Emily's meals were just so ridiculously delicious that she'd trained my palate.

While I thought about it, the man cleared his fourth bowl of ramen.

"Thank you so much for the food," he said.

"No worries. Uhhh…" I realized that we didn't know each other's names, so I introduced myself. "By the way, I'm Ryota Sato. Call me Ryota or Sato, doesn't matter to me."

"I'm Cliff. Thanks, Ryota."

"Are you done already? If that wasn't enough, go on and order more."

"I'm fine now. Really, thank you."

"Okay… So, what's the deal? Have you not been eating?"

I could imagine why, but I played dumb and asked anyway.

"I'm short on cash. It's been three days without meals now."

"Three days? But you should be making a lot of money on dungeon trips, right?"

"We… Oh, well, I have a partner, and we formed a party alongside our captain. The captain manages our finances, and we receive our pay from him."

"And what is your pay?"

"Well…not quite enough."

"Not enough? How much are we talking?"

"Last month was…30,000 piros, I think."

"That's literally pocket money!" I yelled without thinking.

"Huh?" Cliff looked suspicious for a moment.

"Sorry, forget that."

Hey, you're the weird one for looking at me like that.

As a reminder, the common currency of this world, piros, was about equal to yen. For example, the ramen he was eating now was 700 piros per bowl, with an extra 100 piros on top for the large serving.

And he was living on only 30,000 piros a month?!

"How the hell do you live like that—?"

Seeing the look on Cliff's face, I stopped myself and apologized, "Er, sorry."

He *couldn't* live like that. That was how he'd ended up like this.

"What can I do differently? It's because we earn so little."

"Is it going that badly?"

"We get injured sometimes, and our weapons and gear all fall apart constantly. He takes that out of our cut."

"Mgh..."

He takes consumable and equipment expenses out, too?

It might seem logical at a glance, but it was messed up. I mean, his take-home pay was 30,000 for a whole month. That was unthinkable.

Cliff looked extremely dejected.

"Sometimes, I get to thinking that maybe I'm not cut out for this work."

"Really?"

"Maybe there's a place where I'm better suited to work. The captain says I'm being naïve when I bring it up, though."

"That's not true. You're not wrong for thinking that at all."

"But it's the truth," Cliff complained.

"Hm?"

"When the captain picked me up, my stats were in awful shape. My combat stats were low, and my drops were all F except for plants, which were at E."

"I-I see."

That sounded like how Emily was when we'd first met.

In that case...maybe he isn't cut out for this, after all.

"And your drops haven't improved at all?" I asked.

"Huh?"

Cliff seemed surprised.

"Huh?"

So was I.

What does he mean, "Huh?"

"What...do you mean by that?" he asked.

"Uh, exactly what I said."

"Can drops get better?"

"Well, yeah… They can. When you level up."

Cliff froze, gazing wide-eyed at me with his mouth wide open. He forgot to even blink.

So this is what it would look like if they put a picture of "astonishment" in the dictionary...

I remembered the last time I saw him in a dungeon. I remembered the man he called "Captain," the older guy who screamed about dreams.

"Did he tell you…that drop rates could never go up?" I asked him.

Cliff nodded slowly and replied, "Is that not true…?"

"Some people's drop rates never go up, but there's no telling in advance."

At the very least, my friends had their drop rates go up before they capped their levels.

Cliff was astounded.

I paid the bill, and we left the restaurant together, walking through the bustling city.

"Why didn't you ever check for yourself?" I asked.

"The captain always told me not to. He said that looking at your stats would set your limits, and that stats don't tell the entire story. That humans can overcome them."

"That's insane!"

My anger left my mouth before I could stop it. There was some logic there, but that didn't mean you could go on ignoring your stats forever. That man had probably kept him from seeing his stats so that he could control Cliff, who thought himself inferior for having nothing but E-rank plant drops.

I was growing angrier and angrier by the second.

I took Cliff to an item shop in town. There, I bought a portable status board—a consumable item that lets you check your stats—and gave it to him. As the name implied, it was a status board that you could carry. Its effect was the same as the one in dungeons.

"Try using it," I ordered him.

"O-Okay."

As directed, Cliff used the portable status board to display his stats.

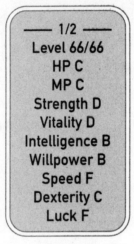

—— 1/2 ——
Level 66/66
HP C
MP C
Strength D
Vitality D
Intelligence B
Willpower B
Speed F
Dexterity C
Luck F

"Look, you've capped your level! How much of a slave driver is that guy?!"

"So these are mine…"

"You're pretty strong, too. Better suited to magic, maybe, but strong."

"Th-Think so?"

"More importantly, go to the next page! That's the one that matters."

"O-Okay."

I heard him gulp nervously. Then, he steeled himself and displayed his drop stats.

—— 2/2 ——
Plants E
Animals F
Minerals C
Magic F
Special F

"…Huh?" he gasped.

Feeling exasperation toward Cliff and rage toward his boss, I declared, "Let's be clear here, stats tell no lies. Your strengths aren't meant to blossom here in Cyclo; you need to be in a place like Indole."

"B-But…"

"There…I'm certain that you could make at least a million piros a month."

Cliff was even more astonished now.

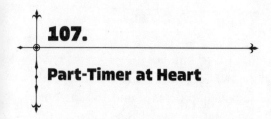

107.

Part-Timer at Heart

"Wh-What's Indole?" Cliff asked me.

"It's a village where a new dungeon was just born. It drops gold dust… Since it's an ore drop, it's perfect for you."

"Huh?" Cliff was surprised.

"Huh?"

Why does he keep getting surprised like this?

"Dungeons can…be born?"

"…What?"

"I-I've never heard of that happening."

"But Nihonium was just born here in Cyclo, wasn't it? And then there's Selenium, which ended up under Cyclo's ownership."

"I-Is that true?"

Cliff looked half-surprised and half-confused. It was common knowledge that dungeons could be born, and Nihonium and Selenium were old news, yet he didn't know either of those?

He'd been exploited all this time, not allowed to know a thing. It made me angry. I was ready to snap, to put it mildly.

"Let me say this one more time—no, I'll say it as many times as it takes. You're better off in Indole."

"B-But…"

"Hah!"

It seemed like it'd take too long to convince him, so I whipped out my guns and fired off combined recovery rounds, creating a sleep round, at Cliff. When it struck him, he fainted and drifted off into the world of dreams.

While Cliff slept, I carried him off to Indole.

In only a few days, Indole had become a place bursting with life. People and products had gathered here, and the citizens were both rebuilding and constructing new things all over the place.

The villagers were cheerful as well. It was clear that this was a blessing wrought by Aurum's gold dust.

"Wh-Where are we…?"

"This is the village called Indole that I mentioned. A picture's worth a thousand words, so let's delve into that dungeon right away."

"Huh? But…"

"Shut up and come with me."

Cliff hesitated, but I pulled him toward Aurum with me.

Just going toward the dungeon was enough to get the villagers to gather one after another and speak to me.

"Oh, our savior!"

"You should tell us in advance if you're coming!"

"Go home and tell Mom. We've gotta prepare for a feast now that our savior's here."

When I told them that we couldn't have a party, since I was here on other business, they all looked disappointed. Seeing them, Cliff's mouth fell open.

"What's the matter?"

"Um, well… Ryota, are you actually a big deal?"

"I'm just an adventurer, though in this village I'm like a Dungeon Association figurehead."

"Dungeon Association?"

Argh, geez! You don't even know what that is?

Now I was getting *really* mad at his jerk boss.

After a while, we made it to Aurum. Adventurers and villagers alike had gathered outside the dungeon. There, I found Alan and called out to him.

"Hey, Alan."

"Savior!"

"What's going on?"

"Oh, you mean all this? Everyone's waiting for the next dungeon entry. Everyone enters together at set times, and we keep people from going in and changing the dungeon layout at all other times."

"I see."

Aurum was a rogue dungeon, so it changed shape each time someone stepped inside. This rule was a way of keeping the dungeon from changing suddenly when people were inside.

That meant I'd be waiting for a while. I decided to leave Cliff for the moment and spoke to Alan.

"How's the village doing?" I asked.

"Wonderful, thanks to you, Savior. Everyone who lived here before is remodeling their homes, and the younger folk who'd been putting off their marriages are finally tying the knot. All of this is because of you."

"I'm just glad things are going well."

"By the way, Savior, my son leveled up, but only his plant drops went up, so we're wondering what to do. It's such a shame that this happened right after he awakened to the joys of dungeoneering."

"Have him come to Cyclo. Hell, I could even help him get his bearings a little."

"Goodness! I could never ask that of you."

"Don't worry about it. He's better off in a place where he can use his strengths."

"Thank you, Savior!"

Other villagers came to speak to me afterward. Given their expressions and tones of voice, it was clear that this village was filled with new vigor and hope.

Once I'd finished chatting with them, I went back to Cliff. For some reason, his mouth was agape.

"What's the matter?"

"How...are you so close with everyone here?"

"Huh?"

"Adventurers are rivals. We watch each other with eagle eyes, always thinking of how we can snatch each other's prey. Never open your heart to anyone but your closest comrades, and be wary of anyone who tries to get too close."

"...I'm guessing your captain taught you that."

Cliff nodded.

Man, he really filled this guy with BS.

I'd heard that cutting off people's connections with others was ideal for brainwashing, but it was even worse to hear it first-hand. The old man really just thought of his partners as slaves.

Everything Cliff said about his so-called captain and the environment he fostered only further fueled my righteous fury.

Once it was time to enter the dungeon, Cliff and I stepped into B1 of Aurum last.

"Whoa!" he panicked. "Everything changed!"

"It's called a rogue dungeon. Every single time someone comes in, the dungeon changes shape."

"I-I see."

"Anyway, look; there's a monster. Go kill it."

"O-Okay."

"Be careful, though," I warned him. "They like to use cheap tricks. No matter what, don't let your guard down until it fades away."

Cliff nodded and took a step toward the little demon. Then, their battle began.

Cliff was an experienced fighter, which was no surprise considering the fact that he was level 66. From start to finish, he kept control of the pace of battle versus this little demon. But just before it was time to finish the monster off, he returned to me.

"Ryota!" he called to me.

"What?"

"Huh? Umm, well…"

"…"

Why did he come to me before killing it? I wondered. But a few seconds later, I remembered why: that was how he'd always done things with his boss.

Cliff and that woman would join forces to weaken a monster, and then, the guy they called captain would finish it off. He was just doing this out of force of habit.

"Not me," I refuted. "You kill it."

"Me…?"

"Yeah. Go finish that thing off."

"…"

Cliff was hesitant. Despite how well he'd fought so far, how he'd overwhelmed the little demon, it began to counterattack.

"What's the problem?" I asked.

"I-I've never finished an enemy off…"

"Tch! Just try!"

"I can't! I can prepare the final blow, but then…"

Cliff was at his wit's end. He was so physically accustomed to holding back and not killing monsters that he couldn't force himself to do it now. Cliff could handle a monster he'd never seen before and bring it near death, but he couldn't deliver that final blow.

The word "spellbound" came to mind.

I thought for a moment and fired a recovery round at the little demon. It struck, healing it. Cliff was able to move again now, so he attacked the healthy little demon once more. Then, just before killing it, he stopped again.

"Kh... What should I do?"

Cliff was at a loss, too. He really could attack just fine until it came to the finishing blow.

In that case...!

I fired another recovery round at the little demon. It healed, and Cliff resumed his attacks.

If I'm right, it took him three attacks before he held back after that last recovery round.

I focused and counted his attacks.

One, two...and three!

I stepped in and fired a normal round between his second and third attacks. My bullet struck first, reducing the little demon's health.

Cliff seemed to notice that, but it was too sudden for him to stop. His third hit overkilled the little demon.

"I...killed it."

"More importantly, look."

As he gazed in astonishment at his hands, I handed Cliff the gold dust that had fallen.

"Wh-What's this?"

"You killed it, so it's your earnings."

"Mine..."

He looked too taken aback to speak as he looked back and forth between me and the gold.

The Indole branch of the Swallow's Returned Favor had finished construction, so I brought Cliff to the new shop. There, I had him call an employee and sell his gold dust.

After that first little demon, I'd continued his rehabilitation by supporting him and making him finish enemies off. In the process, he got more gold dust drops. He had C-rank ore drops, so they didn't drop that often, but he'd still made some money.

Here, he sold them.

A familiar employee, Ina, finished weighing it and returned.

"Thank you for waiting," she said, then placed a few paper bills and coins on a tray and held it out to Cliff. "After taking taxes out, your total is 7,320 piros."

"…Seven thousand piros? I did this?"

"Yeah, you did," I assured him.

Several emotions passed over Cliff's face. Shock. Confusion. Excitement.

"I made all of this…in just one day…"

The fact that he thought it was so much was sad in itself. 7,000 piros was basically a daily wage from a part-time job. It wasn't something that a grown man, with a capped level and C-rank drops, should have to be emotional about.

And yet, to Cliff, a man who'd lived on 30,000 piros a month, it was an unbelievable number.

Eventually, his mind caught up. With raw emotion and joy all over his face, he accepted the money.

"Thanks. This is all because of you, Ryota," he said with a smile.

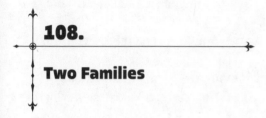

108.

Two Families

The next day, I joined Cliff on another trip to B1 of Aurum. He was still a little awkward in combat, but he'd made great progress. With time, he would get used to farming for himself.

I felt some relief and satisfaction for saving a man from that evil boss.

With his matter settled, I decided I'd return back to Cyclo after we left the dungeon. But while I thought about it, the time came.

A bell rang throughout the dungeon. That clear peal was the sound of a golden bell, made from the same gold mined from Aurum itself. By ringing it at set times, they notified the people inside that adventurers would be entering.

Hearing that, Cliff finished off the monster he was fighting, picked up the gold dust, and came back to me.

"Good job," I said to him. "How are things looking?"

"I think I have even more than yesterday," Cliff said. He put the gold dust he'd gotten so far into his hand and showed it to me. As he'd reported, that was definitely more than yesterday's earnings.

He was level capped and had C-rank drops. And now that I'd cleared the dungeon, the drops themselves were doubled in quantity. One could say it was obvious that he'd make this much.

"Nice."

"This really is all because of you, Ryota."

"Don't sweat it."

I just couldn't sit idly by while someone was taken advantage of.

While we talked, the world around us changed. Each time, Cliff was startled.

"Rogue dungeons are annoying like that," I explained. "Every single time someone comes in, you get taken somewhere else."

"S-So that's just how it works."

"Get used to it, and it can be pretty convenient. See?"

Right on cue, we were taken to the dungeon's exit. Up ahead, we saw adventurers lined up and waiting to enter.

"If you're lucky and have the right timing, you can walk right out."

"That is convenient."

"Ryota!"

Suddenly, someone called my name and hugged me. The world around us changed once more, and we were taken somewhere else in the dungeon.

I took in my surroundings, then looked to see who'd hugged me. It was the princess of boxed air herself, Margaret.

"Margaret?"

"It's been a while, hasn't it?" Margaret replied. She was as soft and fluffy as ever, dressed like a refined and beautiful princess.

"It has. What brings you here?"

"I heard rumors of a new dungeon, so I came to check it out. I'm glad we ran into each other! There's something I've been hoping to show you."

"What is it?"

Margaret looked around, found a status board set up in the dungeon, and ran over to it. I approached and watched her use it.

As she brought up her stats, she turned her soft and refined smile to me.

"Thanks to you, these are my stats now!"

—— 1/2 ——
Level 99/99
HP F
MP F
Strength F
Vitality F
Intelligence F
Willpower F
Speed F
Dexterity F
Luck F

—— 2/2 ——
Plants A
Animals A
Minerals A
Magic A
Special A

"Oooh!"

It displayed the stats I'd expected: at her level 99 cap, her drop rates had all grown to A. Those stats were a lot like how mine were when I came into this world.

☆

127

On B1 of Aurum, Cliff and I watched how Margaret's group fought. That's right, her *group*—she'd formed a party with four dudes. They seemed to match their outfits to Margaret's princess attire, dressing up as four knights.

The four of them attacked a little demon, weakening and cornering it with perfect coordination.

One of them turned and called to Margaret, "Princess!"

Margaret nodded, picked up the same heavy-looking sword she had when I'd first met her, and dealt the finishing blow to the restrained and weakened little demon.

Gold dust dropped with ease, thanks to her high drop stats.

They were like a real Margaret Family. Margaret, with F in every combat stat but A in every drop stat, was supported by her four followers who funneled all the kills to her. This strategy was the result of her stats, appearance, and general vibe.

It was different from the Ryota and Neptune Families that I knew, but just watching them made me certain they'd do just fine together.

Margaret's group continued on to their next target.

Suddenly, I felt something shaking beside me. Cliff, who'd watched with me to this point, gazed at them with a perturbed look on his face.

"What's the matter?" I asked. "You seem upset."

"Is that…okay?"

"Huh?"

"They're acting just like how I used to…"

"…Oh."

Come to think of it, he wasn't wrong. Others weakening a monster, letting only the leader finish it off… Maybe that *was* similar to how Cliff and his former boss did things.

"…" Cliff turned pale, probably reminded of his dark past.

I should say something.

But before I could, the next little demon died, and Margaret picked up her reward. She then turned to her knights.

"Here you go, Lat, Socia, Prey, and Bildar."

She called their names and divided the gold dust among the four.

"Thank you for this blessing!"

All four kneeled at once like real knights and accepted their gifts. The group was a perfect image of a princess and her subjects.

"Huh...? She...gave it to them?"

"That goes to show that Margaret isn't like your old boss."

"Y-Yeah. But why...?"

"Ryota!" Margaret exclaimed, running over and hugging me again while Cliff was stunned. It was almost like a tackle as she clung to my waist and looked up at me. "Did you see my fight?"

"Yeah. You did good!"

"All because of you, Ryota."

"Who are those guys?" I asked.

"They're my Family. When I told them about my stats, they asked if I'd let them fight alongside me."

"So they came to you, huh?"

"That's right."

"And why'd you give them your drops?"

"I wanted to be like you, Ryota."

"Hm?"

"Huh?" Cliff let out a surprised gasp.

"It's because of you that I've come this far," Margaret explained. "You gave me what was yours without reserve, and I wanted to do the same for others."

"I didn't really do much..."

She stopped hugging me, looked up at me from a step back,

and emphatically declared, "That isn't true!1 It's thanks to you, Ryota. No matter what anyone says, even if you won't accept it, I'll keep saying that I owe my success to you."

Her beautiful, refined features had a strong aura—and a measure of firm willpower.

"…Huh. Well, thanks."

"And, um…"

"Yeah?" I urged.

"I would like you to let my Family join the Ryota Family!"

"Mine?"

"Yes!" Margaret exclaimed, gazing at me with a wide smile.

"You want your Family…to be a part of mine?"

She nodded firmly.

Certain phrases popped into my mind. A subsidiary company. A second-generation organization.

"Unfortunately, I cannot fight on my own. There's nothing I can do without those four. As such, I'd like you to let my entire Family join yours, instead of just me."

"I get it. Well, if that's what you want, we welcome you with open arms."

"Thank you! The Margaret Family will now operate under the umbrella of the Ryota Family… We're happy to be with you!"

Overjoyed, Margaret hugged me again.

In the afternoon, we left the dungeon and went to the plaza. Work was progressing well there, too. The remnants of the houses destroyed by Aurum's sudden appearance were gone, replaced with a fountain and various dungeon-related shops in the process of being built.

A weapon shop, an item shop, a drop-buying shop… These

changes made it all too clear that Indole was developing around this dungeon.

It was there that Cliff and I faced each other.

"Well, Cliff, I guess this is goodbye. I'm going home to Cyclo. If you ever need anything, contact me any time."

Cliff's issue was resolved. His misunderstanding of Margaret had been corrected, too; he knew now that she was nothing like that ex-captain of his. And so, I decided to head home.

"Ryota... I mean, Mr. Sato."

"Mr. Sato? Why the sudden change?"

"I want...to join your Family someday, too! There may only be two of us...but please!"

Two of us.

Cliff had a partner, another person who'd withstood the evil boss's abuses to this point. He was saying he'd save her, too.

"Got it. Good luck, Cliff."

"Yes, sir! Thank you!"

Cliff was being awfully respectful all of a sudden. There was no doubt that my actions and Margaret's capacity for kindness had made him decide to rescue his partner.

109.

A Princess's Love

On my way back from Indole to Cyclo, I walked on a paltry road through the otherwise empty wasteland.

Since dungeons dropped everything in this world, moving away from dungeons meant moving away from cities and people and into a lonely, apocalyptic-looking wasteland.

Margaret and I walked through the emptiness together. Unlike me in my adventurer gear, she was dressed very much like a princess—clean, prim, and proper. It made for quite the mismatch with our surroundings.

"So, Ryota, does this mean you're the chief of Indole?"

"There's an actual chief, so no. I'm just the Dungeon Association head, and a figurehead at that."

"That puts you way above the chief. No city or village can survive without dungeons, after all."

"...True, I guess."

Unlike Cliff, Margaret knew the ways of this world well, so her claim made sense.

Cities and villages couldn't survive without dungeons. As such, the leader of the Dungeon Association was much higher in status than a village chief. I could understand that, but I just couldn't think of myself that way. Back in my old world, I was just a regular employee, and my company was so corrupt that new employees never stuck in the past few years, leaving me with no juniors.

I wasn't used to people looking up to me.

"That means you've saved all of them, too," she added.

"I guess so. I rescued them and inspected the dungeon, after all."

And doubled the drops, though I won't mention that.

I wanted to keep the existence of Aurum quiet, whether she was the dungeon's spirit, god, or whatever.

"I'd expect no less of Ryota."

"More importantly…" I trailed off, looked around us, confirmed that nobody was nearby, and asked, "Are those four guys not coming?"

"You mean Lat, Socia, Prey, and Bildar?"

"Yeah."

I think those were their names. Probably.

"They're coming."

"Huh? Uh, where are they, then?"

"Lat," she called.

When Margaret called his name, one of the four knights suddenly appeared diagonally behind me.

"Yes, ma'am!"

"Whoa!" I jumped. He appeared out of nowhere like a ghost, without a sound. He then positioned himself a step behind us, truly playing the part of one who waits upon a princess. "Wh-Where were you?"

"…" Lat remained silent, not answering my question.

"Good question. I wonder…"

Margaret didn't seem to know the answer, either.

Lat showed no willingness to answer me, but he *did* answer Margaret's idle musing.

"We remain far out of the way so as not to disturb you, yet

close enough that we may come whenever you need us, Princess."

"Um, well…there you have it," Margaret said sheepishly.

"Th-That didn't explain anything…"

"Thank you, Lat. That will be all."

"Yes, ma'am!"

Lat bowed and disappeared. I had my eyes on him, but the moment I blinked, he was gone. It was as if he'd never been there at all.

"…Whoa! He didn't even leave footprints!" Only mine and Margaret's were present here. Lat, who'd walked behind us for at least thirty feet, had left no footprints behind. "It's almost like summoning magic. Hell, even better."

"Do you think so?"

"And the way he treats you… I haven't seen someone like that since my older coworker's gofer."

"What is a gofer?"

She doesn't know gofers? I guess that's fair, since she's a princess and all.

"They're underlings who you can order to bring you yakisoba dogs, drinks, and the like."

"Then I think all four of them are gofers."

"Bwuh?"

"Socia. Cold tea, please."

"Here you are, Milady."

This time, another guy appeared diagonally behind Margaret, offering her a glass of tea with ice in it. It was anyone's guess where he'd brought it from. The condensation on the glass was proof of how cold it was, making it look even tastier.

"Whoooa!" I yelped, reeling back in surprise.

"Thank you very much."

"My pleasure, Milady."

The moment Margaret took it, Socia disappeared without a sound. They were dressed like knights, but were these guys actually ninjas?

"That's incredible," I said. "Makes me wonder just how much they can do."

"Do you really want to know?"

"Yeah, a little."

"If you say so…" Margaret mumbled, then came to a stop. "Lat, Socia, Prey, Bildar."

When she called their names, perhaps because she'd stopped, they all appeared in a line in front of her. They then kneeled and bowed deeply.

Ninja background, knightly behavior. The incongruity there was kind of funny.

"How far would you four go to help me?" Margaret asked. In almost no time, yet also unhurriedly, they gave their unfaltering answer.

"We live for Princess Margaret."

"We die for Princess Margaret."

"Princess Margaret's joy is everything."

"All in this world exists for Princess Margaret."

"They're fanatics!" I shouted. "They're religious fanatics!"

"Thank you all," she said to them. With that, the four once again disappeared. "There you go. Is that enough?"

"Yeah, I'm more than convinced now. Oh, but…didn't they accept gold dust from you before? Wouldn't guys like them be too modest to accept it, or something?"

"*Anyone who refuses a gift from Princess Margaret is worthy of a thousand deaths.*"

"Wargh?!" I was so shocked that I jumped.

"What's the matter?" Margaret asked, looking at me in confusion.

I looked around. Someone had definitely just whispered into my ear, but when I looked, nobody was there. And that voice seemed different from normal voices, too.

This is wild. Like, really *wild.*

But as my shock subsided and I calmed down, I found myself accepting it.

"They're real fanatics," I mused. "But y'know, I figured you were kind of like an idol when we first met. You even sold boxed air."

"What is an idol?"

"Huh? Uhhh…the kind of person everyone likes, I guess," I answered with my own lazy interpretation.

"Everyone…likes?"

"Yeah."

"Even you, Ryota?"

"Huh?"

"Do you…like me, too, Ryota?" Margaret asked, looking straight up into my eyes.

My heart skipped a beat. Her flushed cheeks, teary eyes… It was almost as if—

Wait, wait, wait, no! Idols can't fall in love or get married!

"I like you, Ryota…but do you…like me?"

She threw a fastball straight at me. It dealt a critical hit to my heart.

Thump! Thump!

My heart rate spiked.

With tears in her eyes, Margaret gazed at me.

"…"

While I panicked and my heart throbbed, her expression turned to confusion, then sadness. It looked like she was about to cry.

"That's a no, I take it…?"

"No, that's not it!"

"Really?"

"Yeah! I think I like you, but—"

There was the whole kiss with Erza. And hell, I barely had any experience with this stuff to begin with.

I didn't know what to do. And while I wavered, my field of vision darkened, and I felt a soft touch on my lips. It lasted only a tenth of a second, like a baby bird's peck, but it was clearly a kiss.

My mind went blank.

"...Ah! Wh-What have I done?!"

Margaret blushed even more. She was practically steaming red.

"Lat, Socia, Prey, Bildar! Hide my face!"

"Yes, ma'am!"

The four ninja-knights appeared out of nowhere and surrounded Margaret.

"Urrrk... I-I'm so sorry!"

Still embarrassed, she ran off with her hands covering her face, still surrounded by her knights.

I just stood there, mouth agape.

"Sir Sato."

One of the knights who'd been guarding her was suddenly next to me.

"Whoa!"

I think this guy was...Lat? But wait...didn't he JUST leave with Margaret? Why is he right next to me?!

I panicked again, but Lat remained calm. He gazed directly at me, looking mighty serious. The very image of sobriety and earnestness, he said, "I have never seen Princess Margaret so happy."

"Huh? Uhhh..."

I'd expected him to tell me off like, *How dare you do this to our princess, you brazen fool?!* but he did the exact opposite.

"Please continue as you are."

Lat saluted me and disappeared.

"Continue as I am...?"

I recalled the sensation of the kiss. Imagining the feeling sent my heart rate skyrocketing.

110.

New Personal Best

On B5 Nihonium, amidst the falling dungeon snow, another of my limitless lightning rounds missed the red skeleton, struck the wall, and burst.

"Tch... Another miss. I'm below fifty percent now..."

I'd been doing badly all day today. My accuracy rating against the red skeletons started at a sad 0%, and I was finally close to getting over 50%.

I knew the reason well. Even now, I was nervous and distressed.

The red skeleton circled around me and struck me with its bone. It was a clean hit on the back of my head. Its red bones rattled as it laughed at me.

"Don't...underestimate me!" I roared, digging my heels into the ground, tensing up all of my muscles, and whipping around to strike with a backhand blow.

The red skeleton backed off at incredible speed, but I stepped forth, unbothered, and hit my mark. Its skull went flying, smashing to bits against the dungeon wall.

I picked up its seed drop, raised my MP by 1, and sighed to let out all of the air in my lungs. Then, in the dungeon snow, I clawed my hands through my hair and messed it up.

Naturally, I was off my game because of what happened with

Margaret. I still agonized over that sneak attack kiss from yester-day. Thus, in the absolute worst state, I took far longer than usual to farm my daily seeds in Nihonium. I ended up with a crappy 40% accuracy rate.

The long war dragged on until lunchtime, and worse, I didn't even get my MP to the next rank. I trudged out of the dungeon, dejected.

That afternoon, I went to Tellurium alone and ran into Margaret at the entrance.

"Ryota!"

She spotted me and excitedly ran over.

My heart started beating faster and faster, and I let out an, "Urk!"

"I've been waiting for you."

"You have?"

"Yes! I went to your house, but one of your Family members told me that you'd be in Tellurium this afternoon."

"Oh… I see," I said, averting my gaze. My ears were heating up. I couldn't look her right in the eye. Anytime I saw her face, I remembered that kiss. "A-Anyway, do you need something?"

"Yes, actually. I wanted to watch how you farm."

"How I farm?"

"Right. Among all the many adventurers in Cyclo, I'd like to watch the most skilled one. After all, it would be in my best interest to learn how to carry myself in a battle."

"How to carry yourself, huh?"

"The more skilled I am, the easier it should be for my knights."

"Yeah. That would let you respond to more varied situations."

Their strategy was for the guys to weaken enemies and for her to finish them off, but the tactics involved could vary based on who said finisher was.

Being stronger meant that her helpers wouldn't have to bring down a monster's HP as much, while having more accuracy would mean they wouldn't have to restrain the foe. As Margaret grew stronger, they would gain more options.

"…Your aspiration is commendable," I muttered.

"Hmm? What was that?"

"Nothing. Okay, come with me."

"All right!"

Margaret flashed a huge smile and followed me into the dungeon.

When we got to Tellurium's first basement floor, I murmured, "It's kind of moving."

"Huh?"

"I mean, when I first came here, I had stats like yours. My drops were all high, but my stats were all F-rank."

"Really?"

"Yeah."

"Then could I be like you someday?"

Why would you wanna be like me? I wondered for a moment, but that wasn't the thing to focus on.

"Yeah, I'm sure you could."

That reply made Margaret's eyes shine, filling her with hopes for the future. I figured that was what mattered.

And so, I began my usual farming. I pushed my magic cart through the dungeon. A slime appeared and jumped at me. I caught it in my hand and shot it while it was above the magic cart. It pierced the slime and killed it. The bean sprouts it dropped fell in.

"That's incredible!" Margaret piped up. "All that from just

one attack."

"Notice how I killed it above the cart? That makes it so I don't have to waste time picking up the drops. Slimes are weak enough that I can kill them easily, which lets me focus on efficiency."

"I see! That's very useful knowledge!"

I'd also used a normal bullet over a limitless lightning round for the sake of efficiency.

Recently, I'd learned that the lightning strike would burn the monsters to death, which made it take longer to receive the drop. Normal bullets, however, made them drop items as soon as they were pierced through. It was only a difference of a few seconds, but that could build up to a major time loss for lightning rounds.

Convenient for their limitlessness, and powerful as well, the only weakness of lightning rounds was that they weren't optimal for speedrun strats.

With Margaret in tow, I killed slime after slime.

Kill slime, put bean sprouts in cart, search for next slime.

But then, I stopped.

"Is something the matter?" she asked.

"Hold on a second."

Margaret cocked her head.

With guns in hand, I waited a little while. Thirty seconds later, a new slime appeared before us. I instantly killed it and put the bean sprouts in the cart.

"Wh-What was that?"

"Monster spawn points are mostly set. This spawn point produces a slime every five minutes. We did a full lap, so I figured it was about time."

"You've even memorized that?! Amazing!"

"It comes to you with time."

"Is there anything else I should know?" Margaret asked,

amazed. Her eyes shone like an excited child.

I wanted to meet her expectations somehow, so I told her everything I'd memorized and committed to muscle memory. I also demonstrated the most efficient method of farming here in Tellurium. Each time, she squealed in excitement about how amazing it was. That look on her face harbored both beauty and cuteness in high volumes.

And so, I did everything I could to see it over and over again.

In the evening, Margaret and I left Tellurium and walked through town together.

"That was incredible," she complimented me again.

I'd shown her how to defeat each monster, farm them efficiently, and general dungeon strategy from B1 to B7. Margaret was overjoyed the entire time, making me glad I'd gone through the effort.

"Simply amazing, Ryota. That's my prince for you."

"Pri—?!"

Margaret's directness made me nervous again. The nervousness I'd forgotten when I single-mindedly hunted to show her my cool side now washed over me anew. I caught sight of her pink lips.

Oh, no. What do I do?

Now that my mind was on it, and with Margaret herself right in front of me, I grew more and more nervous.

"Oh, there you are. Heeey, Ryota!"

"Huh?"

Hearing a voice, I turned around and saw Alice. She waved and ran over to me with her three chibi-sized monsters sitting on her shoulders. In a way, my savior had appeared.

I pushed any sense of nervousness out of my mind and turned to her.

"What's up?" I asked.

"Urgent news! You probably would want to know this, so Erza sent me to tell you."

"Urgent?"

"Yeah!" Alice nodded firmly and smiled her usual innocent smile. "Congratulations! You made more than three million piros today!"

"...Oh?"

"That's a new personal record!"

"Wow. A new PR, huh?" I mused.

"Three million in a day is huge! How'd you do it?"

"Huh?"

My heart skipped a beat, but it felt different this time. I turned from Alice to Margaret, who looked blankly back at me.

So she doesn't know? Good.

If she knew why, I'd probably die of embarrassment on the spot. I'd spent this morning at less than half efficiency, yet my desire to show off to Margaret in the afternoon had led to a personal record.

"I don't quite understand, but congratulations," Margaret said.

"Congrats! You're so cool, Ryota," Alice added.

Hearing her say that made it feel just a tiny bit more embarrassing.

111.

Farming Magic

On B5 of Nihonium once more, I took down a red skeleton and harvested a seed from it. The seed melted like snow in my hand, and I heard a voice in my mind.

"There it is... S-rank."

I'd been able to tell the progress of my stat growth by feel for a while now. I'd started this morning at A-rank and I'd kept a count of how many I'd defeated so far, so I knew that one should've been the one to bring me to S-rank.

When a new red skeleton appeared, I insta-killed it and turned to leave. Then, I went to the front of the dungeon and stood before the status board.

Nihonium didn't have any inside the dungeon, since people thought it didn't drop anything. However, there was one right outside the dungeon.

I stood there and operated it as usual.

—— 1/2 ——
Level 1/1
HP S
MP S
Strength S
Vitality S
Intelligence F
Willpower F
Speed S
Dexterity F
Luck F

Thanks to the MP seeds from the B5 red skeletons, my MP was at S now.

My fifth S-rank stat. I'd started off with F in everything, but that was no more.

It simultaneously felt like a long time and a short time. Because my other stats had gone up, and I had gathered both normal and cheat items, it had been pretty easy. However…there wasn't any palpable benefit to the increased MP, to the point that I had to say, "I don't really *feel* the increased MP."

I'd felt the increased HP and vitality, since I took less damage, becoming confident that I had no worries of being killed by normal monster attacks. And I'd especially felt the boosted strength and speed when fighting hand-to-hand with monsters.

But the MP? Not at all.

I knew two spells now: Wind Cutter and Reservation. Wind Cutter was level 1 wind magic. The basic of the basics. Reservation made it so that, no matter who killed it, any monster of my choosing would drop an item as if it had been killed with my

S-rank drops.

I didn't use either much, for different reasons. The former was weak, while I only used the latter against strong foes when in a party. Still, Reservation was good. It was very effective when I *did* use it.

Either way, I didn't use much magic now, which meant I didn't get any benefit from S-rank MP.

"Maybe…I should buy magic fruit."

Back in Cyclo, I went to the magic fruit vendor. There, I looked over the three different magic fruits.

"You know, maybe it's not my place to say this…" the shop-keeper, Isaac, said with an affable grin. "but you won't know no matter how long you stare at them. I understand your concern, but nobody can tell what spells will come from a magic fruit until they eat it."

"…You might be right."

Still, I gazed at them, searching for some sort of difference.

I mean, they weren't cheap, everyday goods. A single one cost 3,000,000 piros. It wasn't something that I couldn't afford these days, but that didn't mean I could just throw out that much money on a whim. Basically, for 3,000,000 piros, I was going to buy one; I just wavered over *which*.

Isaac shrugged in surrender and said, "Anyway, you're free to stare at them as long as it takes for you to be satisfied."

He seemed used to this; a lot of customers were probably like me.

"…Mmm."

I stared and stared at the magic fruit.

From the front. From the back.

From the sides, above, and below.

From every possible angle I could.

"Oh!"

Suddenly, when I backed off and gazed at them all at once, I saw something behind the leftmost magic fruit. Not believing my eyes, I rubbed them.

"Is something wrong, sir?" Isaac asked.

"That…"

"That?" Isaac repeated as he looked at the magic fruit I'd pointed at. "Do you have some issue with this magic fruit?"

"…"

I managed to stop myself from saying, *Don't you see it?*

He probably couldn't. It seemed like only I could.

A woman wearing a ceremonial kimono was standing behind the leftmost magic fruit. She was translucent and somewhat bigger than the fruit.

She's almost like a ghost…

"…I'll take this one," I decided.

"Thanks for your business!"

I suppressed the urge to say what I wanted to say and bought the magic fruit in front of the smiling kimono-clad woman.

I went to the outskirts of Cyclo—my usual place when I didn't want people nearby. When I reached my designated outsider generation area, I put the magic fruit on the ground.

I'd stopped seeing the ghostly woman after I left the shop. Before, I might have been confused by the sudden appearance of a kimono-clad woman, but not anymore. As someone who'd met the spirit of Aurum, one possibility came to mind.

Nihonium. A woman in a kimono.

"...Sounds a little too easy, right?" I mused as I waited for the magic fruit to turn.

Normal magic fruits only let a person learn one spell, but if they were turned into outsiders and made to drop again with my S-rank drop stats, they became magic fruits that let you learn two spells. And so, I waited for it, like a chef cooking with high-quality ingredients.

Before long, an outsider burst from the magic fruit. Like before, it was a monster akin to liquid metal that assumed my shape. This monster had 80% of the strength of the person it turned into.

On Metal Ryota's shoulder, I saw the kimono-clad woman for a brief instant.

"There she is again."

She stood on its shoulder like Alice's monster buddies. After smiling, she disappeared. Then, the monster attacked.

Like the last time, I evaded and fired off a fully-buffed restraining round before loading the enemy full of limitless lightning rounds. I was glad to have them. If not for them, it would've taken a whole ton of bullets to deal with this thing.

There were always monsters out there that weren't made to be fought a second time, like this guy, rare monsters, dungeon masters, and the like. Not that I couldn't take them down again, but it was just such a hassle that I'd prefer not to. Part of why I wanted to get stronger was to fight monsters like them.

While I thought about it, the fallen outsider became a magic fruit. The hexagram that had once been on it was no longer alone, as there were now two of them. I ate it, and the effects of two spells popped into my mind.

The first was Magic to Force. When activated, it buffed every physical attack in exchange for consuming MP with each strike. As for the other...

"Sir Sato."

"Wargh!" I jumped, scared by the sudden voice. It was Lat, one of the ninja-knights who served Princess Margaret. "Wh-What?"

"I ask that you lend your aid."

"My aid...? Wait, are you injured?"

He'd scared me, but now that I got a good look at him, Lat was pretty torn up. His armor was dented in some places, and blood was flowing here and there.

"What's going on?"

"Princess Margaret is in danger."

"What?!"

I rushed to B1 of Nihonium.

When I went inside, the air-selling man called out to me, "Mr. Sato!"

"Where's Margaret?"

"There!" he yelled as he pointed in a particular direction. I followed his finger and saw Margaret being protected by three of her knights.

Margaret had fallen and wasn't moving, while the other three had their hands full fending off enemy blows. They had no chance to take her and run.

That was just how cornered they were by the monster. And that was no surprise, honestly. They were fighting a five-foot tall being with hair even longer than its height.

Its body was translucent, like a ghost. This was Nihonium's dungeon master.

"That's an unlucky run-in," I said.

"We didn't think it would appear... Mr. Sato, please do

something!"

"I've got this."

Lat, the one who'd come to find me, stood by me and declared, "I'll do anything. Just say the word."

I glanced at him. Though they were hidden by his armor, his wounds weren't superficial. The blood pouring from him made that much clear. And yet, he didn't shrink back or show any signs of fear.

The look on his face said that he'd do anything for Princess Margaret. I had to be impressed...hell, even *respect* him for that.

"It's okay," I replied. "I'll handle this alone."

"...Can you?"

"Yeah."

Sensing my confidence, Lat remained quiet and left it to me.

I took another step forward and saw her—not Margaret, and not the dungeon master. It was the woman in the ceremonial kimono. She smiled sweetly. Then, a word appeared in my mind, which I repeated to myself. She must have appeared just to tell me that.

"Thank you," I whispered to her.

She smiled again, in satisfaction this time, and disappeared.

I said the word—chanted the incantation—that she'd taught me.

"Repetition."

The moment I used it, incredible fatigue weighed on my body. That was the sensation of losing all of your MP at once.

Figures. You'd need something like that against a dungeon master.

Repetition: a spell that exchanged MP for the ability to instantly kill a monster you've killed before. That was the second spell in the magic fruit that the kimono woman had chosen for me.

The dungeon master of Nihonium, a foe that had once backed me into a corner, fell in one blow in exchange for every last drop of my S-rank MP.

112.

New High-Water Mark

On B1 of Tellurium, a slime appeared. I held my hand out toward it. My hand was empty, holding no gun.

"Repetition."

I used my new magic, which instantly defeated any monster type I'd beaten already.

The slime disappeared and dropped bean sprouts. I picked them up and put them in my cart.

That was the easiest one yet. I never missed slimes with my guns anymore, but I still had to focus when I aimed. Repetition didn't need that; I just had to perceive the enemy I wanted to use it on. And on top of that...

"Didn't use much MP, either."

I'd only used it once yesterday, on Nihonium's dungeon master, in order to save Margaret. That time, I felt immediate fatigue, as if I'd used up all of my MP at once. But today, when I used it on a slime, I was fine.

Another slime appeared, and I used Repetition again. It died and dropped bean sprouts. The MP consumed by Repetition to kill a monster seemed to be proportional to the monster's strength, and slimes consumed almost nothing.

"In a way... Actually, no. It *really is* the strongest magic in this world."

In a video game, this would be something convenient to have. But in this world, I considered it the strongest. Because everything in this world dropped from monsters, dungeon farming was the means of production. The repetition involved in production meant that the ability to consistently defeat monsters was valued above all.

It was no exaggeration to say that magic that could guarantee a monster's instant death was the strongest.

"The problem is…how many times can I use this?"

Slimes didn't cost much MP, but that didn't mean zero. I could slowly feel my MP being drained.

Let's find out how long I can keep this up.

I used Repetition against the weakest enemy, slimes, over and over.

Defeat enemies with magic, receive bean sprouts, bean sprouts go in cart.

Once it was full, I pushed the button and sent it all home.

I repeated this process, fully concentrating on my work.

"…Phew."

Finally, I'd run out of MP. At 3:00 PM in the afternoon, in half the time it usually took to do my daily farming, I ran out. Even with S-rank MP, three hours of nonstop magic-casting would do that to you.

Now, what's the result?

I returned home. It was my first time coming back from Tellurium with the sun still so high in the sky.

"I'm back," I announced as I entered the open area on the first floor of our three-story home.

Erza alone, dispatched to us from the Swallow's Returned

Favor, was there in the shop-like space.

"Welcome home, Ryota," she greeted me with a smile. "You're early today. What's the occasion?"

"I wanted to ask about my earnings so far."

"Oh, I figured!" she replied, grinning.

I cocked my head and asked, "You figured? Why?"

"Ryota, you've started doing something new today, haven't you?"

"Can you tell?"

"I sure can. Your usual way of sending things and your way of sending things when you're doing something special are very different."

"I see."

So even a third party can tell...

"Anyway, here's my passbook."

"Wait just a moment," Erza said as she accepted it and re-corded my daily earnings.

I felt both nervous and excited as I waited. After a while, she finished recording and handed it back to me with a big smile.

"Here you go."

"Let's see... Three million?!"

Today's earnings, as recorded in the passbook, rounded to 3,000,000 piros.

Isn't this...?

"It's exactly the same as yesterday's record, isn't it?" she said.

It was the same amount as when I'd gone all-out and broke through my limits to look good in front of Margaret. The same amount of money, yet in half the time.

"That's incredible, Ryota. You matched your personal record in half the time. Really, *this* should count as your personal best."

"It's all thanks to my new magic."

"Oh? Did you learn a new spell?"

"Yeah, I ate a magic fruit."

"I see... Goodness," Erza mumbled as she gazed at me reverently.

I stared at my passbook, looking at the money that I'd spent yesterday and the money I'd earned today. Considering my new magic and the time I had left until the end of day...

"I'm going back to the dungeon," I declared.

"Again?"

"Yeah. There's only a little under two million left until I've got ten million."

"Oooh!" Erza gasped. "At your current pace, you might just make it in time!"

I smiled back at her.

"Exactly. Here goes nothing!"

"Do your best! I'll do my best to keep up, too!"

She pumped her fist in encouragement, sending me off as I ran back to Tellurium.

I'd used up my MP, but that was no problem. I loaded recovery rounds into my gun and fired them into myself like injections, fully recovering my MP.

Back at full MP again, I returned to the dungeon and farmed once more. As a result, I saw a number that I'd never, ever seen in my old world.

My bank account had ten million piros in it.

113.

Not Alone

At night, I went to the bar Villa di H in Cyclo. This was my favorite joint in Cyclo because they had different beer that was brought in from dungeons all over the world every single day.

With my daytime work done, I'd come to drink with Emily.

"It's been so long since we went out alone together, Yoda!"

"It sure has, huh? We've got more friends around now, so it's rare for us to be alone," I replied as I gulped down my beer and ordered a refill. They had ten different kinds of beer. I liked to drink each one in order, as if I was at a wine tasting. "Eve never wants anything but carrots, and Alice can't drink much. What about Celeste, though?"

"Celeste is resting at home," Emily answered. "She said she has a headache."

"A headache? Is everything okay?"

"She didn't have a fever, so I think she's fine. But I told her to let us know right away if anything happens."

"All right."

The short girl sitting across from me drank beer as well, though she sipped at it slowly. Despite her height, she was an adult. And a hell of a homemaker, at that. If the Family's de facto mother said Celeste was fine, then I believed her.

"Hahaha..." Emily laughed.

"What's so funny?"

"Yoda, you haven't noticed?"

"What?"

"Everyone's been staring at you for a while now."

"At me?"

I put down my glass of beer and looked all around the place. Now that she mentioned it, it did feel like I was getting a lot of attention. Men and women alike were shooting glances my way—though for some reason, the women looked away when I made eye contact.

"You're famous now, Yoda."

"Famous?"

"Yeah! Being with you makes me feel pretty smug."

"Y'know, they might be looking at you instead of me," I rebutted. "Emily Hammers have been flying off the shelves, right? Whenever I take a peek inside Arsenic, more than nine out of ten people have them."

"O-Only because the hammer itself is so good!"

Emily suddenly grew embarrassed, looking down and blushing. I wasn't too used to fame, but Emily was even less hardened to being popular. It was cute when she got all shy, so I decided to be a little mean.

"Don't be modest. You're the number two of the Ryota Family, you know?"

I said that loudly enough for the other people in the bar to hear. People began clamoring, all eyes gathered on Emily.

"That kid is their number two? She doesn't look the type."

"Don't call her a kid, you idiot! That's Emily Brown. People call her the Tiny Giant, the Muscular Holy Mother, and She Who Breaks Rocks in One Swing!"

"Is she that big a deal? Guess you can't judge a book by its cover... Just goes to show how good an eye Ryota Sato has, to pick her as his number two. Or is it a sixth sense?"

Some still focused on me, but now, everyone else was looking at Emily. She grew yet more embarrassed, turning red from her face to even her hands and feet.

I found that downright adorable. I wanted people to know more of the greatness of Emily that I knew, so I extolled said greatness for all to hear.

After complimenting Emily to no end in the bar, I headed home with her.

Cyclo was kind of a sleepless city. Thanks to monsters appearing at all hours of the day and night, adventurers frequented the dungeons even after sunset, and the shops of the busy streets stayed open to serve them.

Even the place we passed through now boasted the same bustling brightness as modern Japan despite it being nighttime. The liveliness here was enough to make me confident that any place in the world could flourish as long as it had a dungeon.

"Hm?" I mumbled as I came to a stop.

"What's wrong?" Emily asked, looking up at me curiously.

My eyes were glued to a certain open-air shop. Or, more precisely, they were glued to a particular adorned mirror among the goods there.

Noticing this, Emily asked, "Did the mirror catch your eye?"

"You can't see it? So then…"

"Do you see something?"

"Yeah," I confirmed, walked over to the shop, and squatted down.

I gazed at the mirror. There was no doubt about it. I rubbed my eyes, but it didn't seem I was just seeing things because of the beer.

A person was sitting seiza-style in front of the mirror—a tiny woman wearing a kimono. She was the same one who'd led me to the magic fruit with Repetition. She didn't say anything, but it seemed like she was telling me to buy it.

I believed she was Nihonium, which meant this mirror was related to it somehow, too. The woman also had a really concerned look on her face.

"Sir, would you like to buy this?"

"…Yeah," I replied. I didn't know why, but I figured I should buy it either way. "How much is it?"

"Fifteen million piros."

"Come again? Fifteen million piros?"

I couldn't believe what I was hearing.

"Yes, sir. This is a treasure from a certain noble's mansion. It has quite the distinguished pedigree."

"So it's an antique, huh?"

"That's right."

Still, fifteen million… I mean, I guess that makes sense if it's an antique from a noble's mansion. A real rich person would probably buy antiques that are that expensive, or let them go, like they're nothing.

"Sure, I'll buy it."

"That's music to my ears!"

"But can you hold it for a day? I'll bring the money around this time tomorrow."

My bank account was only just over ten million. If I used Repetition at full speed, I could make the remaining five million in a bit over half a day. So though I didn't have the money now, I could make that much by this time tomorrow.

"Sure," the seller replied. "But I'm leaving this city tomorrow, so I can't wait any longer."

"Got it. No problem."

"See you tomorrow!"

"Yeah," I replied and looked at the girl in the ceremonial kimono again. She waved to me with a relieved smile.

Based on her reaction, I knew I had to get my hands on it.

The next morning, I woke up and stretched. The weather today was great. As usual, the home maintained by Emily was the very picture of comfort.

I felt great, and it seemed like two sets of my S-rank MP would get me to five million. I left my room and went down to the second-floor living room.

"Huh?"

I spotted Celeste sitting exhausted at the dining table.

"Good morning. What's up, Celeste?"

"Ah… Morning, Ryota."

"Seriously, are you okay? You're super pale."

"I'm fine. It's normal."

"Really? I mean, if you're not feeling well, don't push yourself. We're friends, so if you need anything, I'm more than glad to help out."

"Thanks… You're too nice, Ryota… But I'm fine. It's just a magic storm."

"Oh, okay. So that's why you're not feeling well, and why you had that headache."

"Yeah. So I'm fine."

"All right."

Hearing that put me at ease. Magic storms were a natural disaster of sorts that made it so mages like Celeste couldn't use their magic. They were kind of like atmospheric depressions in my old world. There was no helping that, so I had to agree with Celeste's assessment that she'd be fine as long as she got some rest.

...

......

....

"Aaaaaah!"

"Wh-Why are you screaming, Ryota?"

"Magic storm..."

A magic storm?!

I met Erza on the first floor where she set up shop.

Weather events like these directly correlated with adventurers' sales, so as an employee, she had an idea of the scale and duration of each magic storm. That was why I asked her about it, but she gave the most despair-inducing answer possible: "I hear that the magic storm will last all day."

"This is so bad..." I groaned.

"What's the problem?"

"See, I need to make five million piros by tonight."

"That should be easy for you as you are now!"

"...If not for the magic storm, yeah."

"...Oh!"

It seemed she realized it now, too.

Indeed, making 5,000,000 piros in a day *would* have been child's play for me—if only I could use Repetition to instantly kill monsters. Normally, with my guns and hand-to-hand combat, I would make two million in half a day. Or three, if I was trying hard to impress a girl. But in a magic storm, I couldn't make five million.

"Th-That is bad..." she agreed.

"...I'll just have to do what I can. Guess I'll pass on my morning Nihonium farming and head straight to Tellurium."

"Understood. I'll do my best to support you!"

"Thanks!"

I went into Tellurium and killed monster after monster. Thanks to the magic storm, there were fewer adventurers than usual and therefore more monsters to kill. And so, I went as hard as I could, mainly using limitless lightning rounds. I occasionally threw in homing rounds, since I didn't have to aim with them.

I used my drop-absorbing pouch as well, positioning it on top of the magic cart so I could transfer drops right away. On top of that, I also used my knowledge of monster spawn points and timings to construct the most efficient route possible.

Thus, I steadily progressed from B1 down, and after clearing B7, I ran straight back up to B1.

Over and over, I repeated this process until noon came.

"You made 2,003,000 piros this morning..." Erza mumbled apologetically. She was considerate enough to come to the dungeon and deliver the bad news herself.

Two million... That's not enough.

One could call that my limit: two million piros in half a day, without the use of magic. My current equipment, knowledge, and abilities could only earn that much.

Normally, that was fine. I'd have been over the moon making 4,000,000 piros per day. But right now, that wasn't enough. I had to make five million by tonight.

"Phew..." I sighed, exhausted.

"A-Are you okay, Ryota?"

"Yeah, I'm fine. Just getting pretty tired."

"I'm glad you're fine. But at this rate..."

Exhausting myself in the morning would naturally mean that I'd slow down in the afternoon.

What do I do?

"Umm... If you'd like—"

Before Erza could say something, two girls entered the dungeon behind her. They were Emily and Alice.

"Emily, Alice. What's up?" I greeted them.

"We're here to help, Yoda."

"Now that we're here, it's gonna be okay!"

"You two...?"

What's going on? I wondered to myself.

Just then, Emily set down her giant rucksack—the same one she'd carried when we first met. She pulled a few things out and began setting them up in the dungeon. A table, a couch, various ingredients... Before long, she'd built a lounge in a corner of the dungeon. It was even equipped with the unique warmth of an Emily home.

"Thanks for waiting," she said. "Take a short break here."

"A break?"

"Take a break, and it'll give you the power you need to keep on running to the end."

"Emily..."

I was touched.

Alice chimed in, "Leave the rest to me."

"Alice?"

"Yep! With me here, it'll be easier to find monsters that aren't already in battle."

"Oh, right! Your skill from being born in a dungeon!"

"Yep! Even you can't tell for certain, after all."

"Right."

I judged monster spawns based on memory and experience, while Alice's unique skill could find them like a radar. With her support, my efficiency would be even higher.

"Emily, Alice…"

"The tears can wait. For now, rest."

"And hunt monsters!"

"…Yeah!"

Alice was right. Now wasn't the time to be moved. I needed to recover as best I could and then spend the afternoon farming my butt off.

I sat on the couch and gazed at Emily and Alice as I relaxed.

"Thanks," I said to them.

They smiled back.

"Not a problem!"

"We're friends!"

Thus, with Emily and Alice's support, I raised my pace in the afternoon and made the remaining 3,000,000 piros.

I had made it to 15,000,000 right on time.

114.

Limit Break!

After successfully buying the mirror, I went with Emily and Alice to Nihonium.

"Thank you both so much."

"Don't mention it!"

"This might be the first time I've helped you, Ryota!" Alice exclaimed as she hopped around excitedly, and the three chibified monsters on her shoulders were just as happy.

"You seem so happy, Yoda. Did you want it that badly?"

"Yeah. Now that I have it, I can really tell…"

I raised the mirror aloft as I walked. Unexplainable feelings rose up from the depths of my heart. I was glad that I had this, even if it meant pushing myself.

This was fate. If I'd let this pass me by, my fortunes would've changed. I couldn't explain it logically, but I was certain of that.

"So hey, what is that?" Alice asked.

"I don't quite know, myself. I just know it's related to Nihonium."

"How do you know?"

"You might understand this, Alice. You know how Aurum's drops doubled after I cleared it?"

"Yeah, I remember."

"That was because I met a spirit named Aurum who was living in the dungeon. When I saw this mirror, I saw the spirit of Nihonium, too."

Alice's eyes opened wide and she asked, "Is that for real?"

"Yeah."

"Huh… So you really had to get it."

"Yeah… Thanks so much, girls."

"You said that already! We're friends, so you don't have to keep saying it," Alice replied, though she put her hands to her cheeks and blushed happily.

"She's right. We're just happy that we could help you, Yoda," Emily added. I could hear the pitch of her voice creeping higher than usual at the end of that sentence, though.

Either way, this was thanks to them.

Holding the fruits of our efforts, we arrived at Nihonium. Adventurers already rarely came this way, but it seemed even lonelier at night.

"Th-This place…is really scary at night," Alice murmured as she held her arms and quivered. "I wonder if something's gonna pop out."

"Pop out?" I asked.

"Like a ghost, or something…"

"Ghosts? Heh, I guess it does kinda feel like that."

"There's no need to worry," Emily said.

"Huh?"

Emily slowly approached Alice and stood on her tiptoes, took the chibi skeleton off her shoulder, and showed it to the girl. "You have Boney on your side, remember?"

"…Oooh!"

"True. Alice already has an undead monster with her."

"Oooh! So if something came out, it would just be like Boney anyway!"

The Boney in Emily's hand pumped a fist and showed off its

eager side.

I doubt that's quite right, but if it makes Alice feel better, then sure. That works for me.

Before long, we entered the dungeon.

"The inside is the same as ever," I mused.

"It's as relaxing as home."

Emily herself fit that description better in my opinion, but I didn't say anything.

"Now, the mirror. What do we—?"

What do we do with it? I tried to say, but it began glowing on its own. It was so bright that it lit up the dungeon as it rose out of my hands.

"Ryota?"

"Let's see what comes out of this…"

I put my hands on both guns. If this was anything like Aurum, I'd have to fight something big first.

Emily and Alice prepared for battle, too. Emily readied her hammer, which was quite a bit bigger than herself, and Alice had her three buddies get into battle-ready mode.

The three of us waited and waited, but nothing appeared. As the mirror floated midair, two items without physical form appeared next to it.

"That's a sword."

"And this one…is a weird shape!"

"…A magatama," I said.

"Magatama?" Alice repeated, cocking her head in confusion. I nodded back.

The physical mirror I'd previously held, along with the hologram-like sword and magatama, reminded me of something. The phrase *Three Sacred Treasures* popped into my mind—perhaps because this dungeon was Nihonium, the element named after Japan.

Kusanagi no Tsurugi. Yata no Kagami. Yasakani no Magatama. Any experienced gamer would've seen those names before, since they were often super important items.

The girl in the kimono appeared in the mirror. I was becoming more certain that she was the spirit of Nihonium by the second.

Nihonium said nothing; she just offered a mature smile.

The sword and magatama, along with the mirror I'd brought, disappeared.

"Th-They're gone!" Alice shouted.

"They took the mirror with them…" Emily added.

"It's fine. This is where it belongs. Seems to me like she's waiting for me to bring the other two items."

"Oooh!"

"That's a shame. So nothing happens unless we bring all three?"

"Not necessarily."

"Huh?" Emily and Alice both piped up, confused.

"Alice, can you point us to a skeleton on this floor?" I asked.

"Umm, I can… Why?"

"Lead the way. I wanna do a quick farm."

"Okay. Follow me," Alice said before returning her now-chibified monsters onto her shoulders. Then, she began walking.

"Yoda, what happened?"

"You'll see."

I grinned at Emily, loaded my limitless lightning round, and followed Alice.

Outside of Nihonium that night, we three stood in front of the status board.

"All right, here goes," I announced.

"Yep."

"Okay."

I reached for the status board and tapped on it.

—— 1/2 ——
Level 1/1
HP SS
MP S
Strength S
Vitality S
Intelligence F
Willpower F
Speed S
Dexterity F
Luck F

The stats that appeared were even more evolved than before: my HP was at SS-rank.

"What the heck? What is this?!" Alice piped up.

"Your HP is SS. Double S... Did that skeleton raise it?"

"Yeah."

"Wow. Is that what the mirror does?"

"I don't quite think so," I disagreed.

"Huh? What do you mean?"

"There are nine stats, right? And Nihonium asked me—well, asked for three items. In other words..."

Emily understood quicker than Alice because she'd known me the longest.

"Can three of your stats go to SS now?"

I nodded in response.

Right, three per sacred treasure. Three times three makes

nine. As a result of giving Nihonium the mirror, three of the seeds' stat caps—HP, strength, and speed, symbolizing the first three floors of the dungeon—had risen to SS.

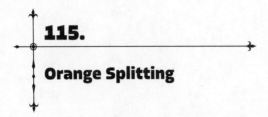

115.

Orange Splitting

The next morning, I went down to B2 of Nihonium, where I mowed down zombies at lightning speed with Repetition.

By using this ultimate farming magic, I instantly killed each zombie that appeared, and their drops were sucked into my pouch.

I raised my stat in half the time it normally took. Just in case, I went outside and checked the status board.

—— 1/2 ——
Level 1/1
HP SS
MP S
Strength SS
Vitality S
Intelligence F
Willpower F
Speed S
Dexterity F
Luck F

Indeed, my strength was now SS as well.

When I went down to B1 of Arsenic, I spotted Emily right away.

She looked surprised when she saw me, but then, she trotted over with her hammer slung over her shoulder.

"Did something happen?" she asked. "It's rare for you to go somewhere other than Nihonium in the mornings."

"My strength went up."

I'd glanced around us and avoided saying it was SS now. It was a secret between my friends and I that my stats could go above A.

In this world, most people had maximum stats of A-rank. That was true of both combat and drop stats. I'd asked Emily first and confirmed with others after the fact, and it seemed certain now. I mean, everyone acted like it was common sense, anyway.

While people were around us here in Arsenic, I spoke vaguely to avoid letting anyone know that my stats could go to S—or rather, SS now.

Almost all of the adventurers here were using Emily Hammers. And now that Emily had come running over to greet me, some were glancing our way. They were probably all Emily's fans, or something. As such, we had to pick our words more carefully.

"It went up? That was fast. Normally, it takes you all morning."

"Repetition and the pouch sped it up. It went a lot faster than usual, so now I'm here to test the change."

"I see!"

Arsenic was kind of a special dungeon. All of the monsters here were rocks. They were extremely tough, limiting the ways you could defeat them. But in return, they never attacked.

It was paradise for hammer-wielders like Emily.

Other adventurers—young, old, man, and woman alike—
were here as well, all those who trusted in their raw power and
broke those rocks. It was the perfect place to test my strength.

"May I watch your test of strength, Yoda?"

"Of course you can."

"Thank you!" Emily exclaimed, sounding as happy as a
kid with a new toy. She *looked* like a kid too, given her height,
though the sight of her hopping around with that enormous hammer would make any man go pale.

I stood with said girl in front of a monster. It was a giant rock,
with eyes and a mouth in the center. This was the dante rock,
Arsenic's B1 monster.

Even when we stood right in front of it, it didn't attack, so I
put a hand to my chin in thought.

"Now, what to do?" I wondered aloud.

"About what?"

"Well, I was able to break these before."

Seeing that there were plenty of other rocks around us, I ca-
sually smacked it. My fist flew through the air like the punch of a
child lashing out, but I put some good force behind it.

Crack!

It broke, and out dropped a dandelion.

"I can do this already," I explained. "So unless I change my
methods. I won't know how much I've grown."

"That makes sense. Can you shatter it?"

"Shatter?"

"Yes!"

"…Hmm. Let's give it a try."

After a moment of thought, Emily and I walked over to the
next rock. As usual, it didn't move or attack. It just sat there,
staring at us as we stopped in front of it.

I took a deep breath. Then, I unleashed a flurry of punches

upon the dante rock, battering it much like I'd seen in a movie—I think there might've been some "star" or "world" punches.

There were some imperfections in my unpracticed technique, but because I punched for twenty straight seconds...

"Wow! You've shattered the rock into tiny bits! It's like sand now."

Emily hopped excitedly again.

Before the rock could turn into a drop, my flurry of punches had blown it to smithereens.

"Hmm... Still not feeling it," I said. "Now that I think about it, I might've been able to do this before."

"Maybe you're right..."

"Any other ideas?"

"I wonder..." Emily mumbled, crossing her arms and cocking her head.

Sure, I'd smashed a rock with my bare hands, but that didn't tell us anything. S-rank was already higher than any other adventurer in the world, and this went even further beyond. It'd be hard to test...but maybe that was to be expected.

Emily and I stood in front of the rock together with our heads resting on our hands, thinking to ourselves.

I slapped it, poked it, and since the monster never attacked, we were free to mess with it as we pleased.

"Do you think you could *squish* it, like a tomato?"

"You really emphasized that—wait, a tomato?"

"Yes?"

"...Huh. That could work."

"You mean the tomato?"

"No, not the tomato. Just watch."

I faced the rock once more. Then, I held out both hands and grabbed its sides. After that...I pressed down.

With a hand on either side, I pressed my thumbs down from

the top.

Before long, *crack*, there was a satisfying sound as it broke clean in two.

"Wow! That was like a mandarin orange!" Emily said, excited.

"Right?"

It *had* felt like peeling an orange. You put your thumb into the little hole, and then break it right into two halves. I'd just done that with the rock.

"That was clever, Yoda! I wouldn't have thought of that."

"I thought of it because you mentioned tomatoes. Yeah, I doubt I would've been able to do this before."

Emily picked up the dandelion it dropped and tossed it into the magic cart. Then, we moved to the next rock. Like the last one, I broke it by imagining breaking an orange in half.

"You did it again!"

"I can definitely feel the increase in strength now. Thanks, Emily."

"I didn't do anything. You thought of the incredible feat on your own."

Suddenly, she clapped her hands together. She must've had an idea.

"What's up?" I asked.

"What about trying…them?"

"Them?"

"Steel slimes!"

"…Oooh!"

Emily and I went down to B8 of Tellurium, which was crawling with metallic slimes.

Now this is a worthy test.

After all, when I'd first defeated one, I had to do it by using a freeze round followed by a flame round to create a stress fracture. This would be an even more difficult test of strength than the rocks.

"Okay, here goes nothing!"

"Fight on! You can do it!"

Backed by Emily's cheers, I faced a single steel slime. It targeted me and jumped over for a tackle.

It was pretty forceful, especially given its metallic form. Taking its attack head-on would be like getting hit with a metal ball. A formidable monster, indeed.

I caught it with a single thrust-out hand and squeezed tight. I then clenched both hands on it despite its struggling and put both hands on the top of its head.

Plink! There was a light, metallic noise as it cracked in half like an orange.

"I knew you could do it! You're incredible, Yoda!"

While Emily cheered once more, I caught a second steel slime mid-tackle and broke it the same way.

Seeing its metal body in two halves, I began to recognize that I had SS strength now.

116.

He Who Predicted SS Speed

On B3 of the limestone-cavern-like Nihonium, I hunted mummies covered in bandages.

When I first started out, I'd struggled against their toughness. I looked back nostalgically on when I had to use flame rounds to take advantage of their weakness when normal bullets failed me.

"Repetition."

They were too easy now. Since I'd defeated them before, my ultimate farming magic killed them instantly.

Repetition was easy to use. Pick a target, cast it, and they're dead. If I was in an action RPG to this point, then Repetition made it a turn-based one. It was just that easy to farm now.

"…"

A new mummy ambushed me from the wall. I readied my guns and charged in, strung a knee strike into a roundhouse kick, and then fired a volley of normal bullets to follow up. The charge, physical strikes, and following combo worked perfectly.

I was worried that using Repetition so much might have dulled my skills, but it seemed not.

Yeah. Can't get overconfident.

Repetition could only defeat monsters I'd already defeated, after all. It was even more useless than Wind Cutter against enemies I'd never fought. Looking to my future, I knew I'd still encounter a lot of new enemies.

Each floor's rare monster, each dungeon's dungeon master, the boss before each spirit… I'd have plenty of run-ins with them. Relying on Repetition too much and letting my battle senses dull would be foolish.

Don't be lazy.

I put a light prohibition on Repetition and used the rest of my time here to kill mummies with gun-fu. I fought them as if training, refusing to use even my limitless lightning rounds.

After a full morning of work, I managed to raise my speed from S to SS.

As I walked through Cyclo with Emily, I held my gun out in front of me, pointing it to the side, and pulled the trigger.

Bang—Fsssh…

It fired a normal bullet, which I caught with my free hand. I'd pinched it between my thumb and pointer finger, as if grabbing a bean.

That's right: I'd caught a bullet in midair.

"Wow! How did you just catch that?!" Emily piped up.

"I just moved fast, is all. The moment I fired, I moved my hand faster than the bullet."

"Geez, that's *too* fast. And catching such a speedy object with your hands… I hadn't thought of that."

"I saw something like it in a movie."

"Movie?"

"You wouldn't get it."

Movies aren't a thing in this world, huh?

I pulled the trigger again and caught a second bullet. Bullets were really fast, but my SS-rank speed was even faster. I also knew the timing, since I was firing them, making it even easier to catch the bullets.

"You're going to get even stronger, Yoda. That's incredible."

"Well, my intelligence, willpower, dexterity, and luck still have a ways to go, since I haven't raised them at all yet. Plus, I still have to find the sword and magatama."

"That's okay. I know you can solve any problem, Yoda."

"Thanks."

I didn't know whether I could or not, but if asked whether I'd *try*, the answer was a resounding yes. And so, I farmed small-fry monsters by hand instead of relying on Repetition to maintain my battle senses.

Countless battles lay before me, between raising my remaining stats and solving all kinds of problems.

Raising stats. Receiving items. Those were important too, but I still needed to cultivate an aptitude for battle that *didn't* have anything to do with my stats.

Emily smiled, looked up at me, and said, "I'll do my best alongside you, Yoda."

I was struck by her smile for a moment, but I managed to avert my eyes.

"We don't know what might happen and when. Let's both do our best."

"Okay!"

Still secretly soothed by Emily's smile, I walked alongside her through town until, suddenly, I stopped.

"Yoda? What's wrong?"

"...Look," I said as I raised a hand and pointed to a place nearby.

Clint was there. He was sitting at a café terrace seat with sugar cubes piled on the table. The madman was eating them straight.

Crunch, crunch, crunch...

Clint sighed and muttered to himself, "Oh, I wish someone could do something..."

Emily and I looked at each other. That was theatrical. Like, *too* theatrical.

"How about we take a detour today?" I suggested.

"I think that would be for the best," Emily agreed, and we turned around to go back the way we'd just come.

We didn't know what might happen or when, so we prepared for that.

Clint and I had a mutually advantageous relationship, so I was ready to help if he needed something—but only if he asked me.

"Y'know, when people wait for you to ask what they want..."

"It definitely feels bad."

Emily and I were in full agreement, so we turned around to leave.

However, Clint stood in our path! He was on the stairs in front of some home's door with sugar cubes in hand, still crunching and munching on them. But now, there were more of them. Before, there was a five-level pyramid, but it had extended to ten levels now.

He sighed ostentatiously again and said, "Oh, I wish there were some strong adventurers around..."

"Emily, how about we just head home for the day?"

"Good idea... I think it would be best if we went home and relaxed."

We made our way home, fast-walking this time.

This is bad. This is clearly very *bad.*

His theatrical wording, his getting ahead of us, the drastic increase in his sugar cubes... Every factor was pointing to the severity of the situation.

We hurried. Our fast-walk turned into a jog.

"We just need to get around this corner, and we're home safe!"

"Yeah!"

We looked behind our backs. Clint wasn't there.

"Did we…shake him off?" Emily asked.

"Emily, don't say that, or else—"

Whenever someone said that, things took a turn for the worse. Like when you've just unleashed your full power on a strong enemy and someone asks, "Did we get them?"

It did not take long at all for it to come true…because when we turned the corner, Clint was right there!

He sat in front of our house…and the sugar cube stack had become a twenty-level pyramid.

"Oh, I wonder if there's anyone strong with high drop rates named Sato out there?"

"Now he's *literally* asking for me!"

After saying that, I immediately panicked and covered my mouth, but quickly gave up. I was trapped either way.

He'd chase us no matter what. Even if we ran away today, he'd be back tomorrow—hell, even if we'd escaped into our home, he'd be two steps ahead of us.

We couldn't escape, so I resigned myself and spoke to Clint.

"What's the problem?"

"Oh, Sato, perfect timin—"

"Cut the act, please," I interrupted him. "What happened?"

I already decided I'd take on the task, so I figured we should just omit the back-and-forth.

"…First, thank you," Clint gazed into my eyes and said that with the serious face of the Dungeon Association head I knew all too well. "I couldn't ask anyone but you for such an important thing."

This was the most serious I'd ever seen him.

"Arsenic…is dying."

117.

The Immovable Object

Clint and I faced each other in the meeting room of the Dungeon Association, where he nervously chewed on his sugar cubes. He chewed them when we came into the room, he chewed them after speaking with his secretary, and he chewed even when he sat down. He just gobbled down that giant pile of sugar cubes like some kind of rodent. It was so much that I got heartburn just looking at him.

"You sure can eat, huh?" I mused.

"Apologies for showing you such an unpleasant side of me."

"Is it related to Arsenic dying?" I asked. Clint nodded firmly, still chewing on his sugar cubes. "Tell me what's going on. How did you learn that the dungeon was dying?"

Clint gazed at me for a while before sighing and swallowing all of the sugar in his mouth. He then said, "It looks like bringing this to you was the right decision."

"Why's that?"

"Your question just now. You are fully aware that dungeons die, and you don't question that fact."

"...That's just one of the rules of our world, isn't it?"

I played dumb. In a way, that was a careless mistake. The reason I didn't find that claim confusing was that I'd already met Aurum and Nihonium. It was therefore easy for me to accept that

186

dungeons die. However…

"In that case, you should be aware of the Sanguine Shower. After all, everybody who knows of dungeon death knows that."

"Sanguine Shower… Like a rain of blood?"

"Right. It happens within a dungeon when said dungeon is near death. Blood falls on the various floors. However, it's only a visual phenomenon; it doesn't actually touch the people inside."

"So it's like dungeon snow," I noted.

"Yes. Sanguine Showers and dungeon deaths come as a pair. None know only one or the other."

"I see."

"You are a mysterious man, Sato. If there's anyone who can stop Arsenic's death, I have to believe it's you and you alone."

There wasn't any point in asking *why* Arsenic's death had to be prevented. In a world where all items came from dungeon drops, dungeons had untold effects on a city's tax revenue. As the head of the Dungeon Association, Clint would naturally want to prolong their lives.

On the other hand…

"Is it normally impossible?" I asked.

"…Right. Nobody's ever been able to prevent it."

"Got it."

I stood up and headed for the door.

"Are you going to do it?"

"I can't make any guarantees, but I'll test out a few ideas."

"Thank you! Thank you so much!" Clint stood up, followed after me, and shook my hand over and over as he repeated his thanks.

I went down to B1 of Arsenic. When I stepped inside, I was

shocked by the sight before me.

Sanguine Shower. Literal raining blood. While the gentle fall of dungeon snow from other floors was almost a dreamy sight, the red rain here made for a dreadful mood. Its one salvation was that it had no physical effects, much like dungeon snow.

"First, I'll have to go and meet Arsenic," I said and turned around.

There were four girls behind me: Emily, Celeste, Eve, and Alice. The whole Ryota Family had gathered here.

"How do we do that?" Emily asked.

"I'm not sure, but when I think back on Aurum, I'd say a path should be opened once we've cleared the dungeon and defeated the rare monster on the final floor."

"Rare monster on the final floor... The Absolute Rock on B30?" Celeste surmised.

"Do you know about it, Celeste?"

"Yep. It's a tough one, too. Though it doesn't attack like all of Arsenic's other monsters, it's so hard that no adventurer has defeated one yet."

"As tough as its name would suggest, then, huh?" I mused.

Can I defeat such an enemy? No, stop thinking like that.

"For now, let's just go try."

"What should we do?" Eve asked.

"Help me clear it. In the worst-case scenario, I might have to clear every floor on my own, but maybe we can split up the work."

"Like with Aurum!"

"That's right, Alice. So..."

I gazed at the four of them. Emily, the tiny girl with a big hammer. Celeste, the long-haired woman who looked even more like a model in the blood rain. Eve, the girl with the bunny suit and natural bunny ears. Alice, who had all three monster buddies on her shoulders.

I bowed my head to all of them and said, "Please help me."

"Leave it to us, Yoda!"

"I-I'll do whatever it takes for you, Ryota."

"Carrots. One heaping helping, and one magic cart helping. Sashimi and steak alongside them, too, please."

"We're fighting as a full Family force! Oh, I'm so excited!"

The friends I'd made in this world each replied in their own special ways. Thanks to them, I was reassured and happy.

We decided to split up the work. Emily, Celeste, and Eve would work together on the first fifteen floors, while Alice and I would do the sixteenth onward.

We went down to B16. When I ran into a monster, I instantly killed it with an annihilation round. These worked better on Arsenic's rocks than my limitless lightning rounds did.

I killed it in one blow, threw the flower it dropped into the magic cart, and sent it right away to Erza back at home.

I didn't know how exactly it would determine whether we'd "cleared" the floors, but I hypothesized that it involved killing, getting drops, and selling them, so I did just that as a set each time.

"Alice!" I called out.

"Got it! The next floor is this way!"

I didn't usually farm Arsenic, which meant that I didn't know where the stairs were at all. Killing the monsters instantly wouldn't mean much if it took me forever to find the stairs, so I'd brought Alice with me.

She guided me onward with her dungeon instincts, and we arrived at B17. I killed the motionless rocks there, too, amidst the bloody rain. After that, I sent the flowers they dropped back home and pressed on.

Arsenic wasn't really a dungeon to be "cleared," honestly. Big rocks, small rocks, floating rocks, buried rocks, transparent rocks, rocks in tiny pieces. There were all kinds, but every single one of them was immobile.

The moment I saw them, I defeated them with annihilation rounds and ran down to the next floor.

Thanks to Alice's guidance, we reached B30 in no time. There, I was about to try annihilating a rock that I happened to see nearby.

"Ryota! Over there!"

Alice pointed the other way, having noticed a presence before me. Amidst the bloody rain stood a particular rock. It was smaller and plainer than all the others around it.

But it was clear that it was...different. And if something was different in a dungeon, that could only mean one of two things, and the fact that there were other monsters around narrowed that down to one.

This was the rare monster of Arsenic's B30, the Absolute Rock.

"You can do it, Ryota! If you beat that thing, I know it'll work!"

"Will it?"

"Yeah, I know it!" Alice replied with certainty. That wasn't just encouragement; she was sensing something, thanks to her dungeon instincts. That was what made her so certain, which reassured me.

I stepped forth and readied my guns, firing a fully-buffed bullet from both guns: one flame round, one freeze round. They fused in midair, becoming an all-engulfing annihilation round. It landed and became a dark orb that swallowed up all of the space around it. However…

"I-It didn't work?" she gasped.

"Seems like it."

The dark orb that had previously annihilated all within had itself been swallowed like a lunar eclipse. After the bullet's effects faded, the Absolute Rock stood there unshaken.

"Ryota, can you do it?"

"…I'll try a few things."

I fired several bullets at the Absolute Rock: fully-powered lightning rounds, piercing rounds, homing rounds, even single flame and freeze rounds. Wondering if this might be a sudden curveball, I also tried recovery and restraining rounds. I even tried combining recovery rounds to make a sleep round. And for good measure, I'd attempted some fully-buffed regular bullets.

Everything failed. I'd tried every single bullet I had, yet the Absolute Rock didn't so much as budge.

"Yoda!" called a familiar voice. I turned to Emily. Her, Celeste, and Eve came running after their completion of the first fifteen floors. "We've finished the upper floors."

"So that's the Absolute Rock," Celeste said.

"Out of the way. The bunny will handle this," Eve declared and slowly walked toward the rock. She raised her right hand and unleashed her slowest chop yet—or rather, her fastest chop yet, which was so fast that it looked slow, but… "…Ow."

It didn't move an inch; worse, Eve's hand made a gross, wet noise and became covered in blood. She didn't show the pain on her face, but there was evident disappointment in its place.

I fired a recovery round at her to heal her hand.

"I'll give it a try," Emily said as she took her hammer and walked away from the Absolute Rock.

After she'd put enough distance between them, she turned around and dashed toward it. With the fastest approach she could muster, she jumped into the air and swung her giant hammer down.

Unlike Eve's repeated strikes, this was a single powerful blow. The cave shook so much that it was difficult to stand. And yet, the Absolute Rock was still intact.

"I-It's still not doing anything..."

"...Say, Ryota, what about that stress fracture stuff you were talking about?" Celeste suggested, with all the perception of a mage.

"You mean heating and then cooling it?"

"Yeah. Would that work?"

I reloaded my guns. Both of them were nearly full of buffing rounds. One had a flame round, and one had a freeze round. That was the same as when I used the annihilation round, but instead of firing simultaneously, I fired one at a time.

Flames enveloped the rock. A second later, a freeze round cooled it all at once. Eve jumped in at the same time, unleashing a super slow chop.

That still didn't work. The rock was unblemished.

"This thing is incredible... Nothing hurts it at all."

"I knew it would be tough, but this is something else," Celeste mused.

"This is bad," Emily chimed in. "If we can't defeat this monster, we won't be able to save this place..."

"If it was a carrot, I could just gnaw it to death..."

My friends were at a loss.

It didn't move. If we wanted, we could escape it by walking away, but its toughness made it the strongest enemy we'd fought yet.

We'd tried everything we had. Was there nothing we could do?

Just then, I noticed something and gasped. It looked like the rock was crying.

In the Sanguine Shower that should have had no physical effect on it, the rock's face seemed to shed tears of blood.

It symbolized the face of Arsenic. The emotions of Arsenic. That was what I gleaned from it.

"Yoda?" Emily asked, surprised as I walked toward the rock.

I put my guns away. They wouldn't work. I stood in front of the rock, closed my eyes, and took a deep breath. Then, I balled up a fist—and punched it as hard as I could.

It did nothing. There wasn't a crack, let alone so much as a chip. Still, I kept punching. Punching, punching, and punching some more. It was as if I was punching something immovable, like a mountain itself. And yet, I punched on and on.

My greatest weapon, my greatest trump card, was this. My last resort: SS-rank strength, derived from having broken the limits of humanity twice—once from being transported to this world, and once more from offering the mirror to Nihonium.

With that, I single-mindedly punched and punched.

"Keep it up!"

"You can do it, Ryota!"

"Go-ooo, go-oooooo, low level."

"We're here with you!"

With my friends' cheers at my back, I punched endlessly. I didn't know how many times I'd done it by now, but I didn't stop, for the rock's tears had disappeared.

Arsenic's monsters always stared at you expressionlessly. But now, this one seemed to be smiling, so I kept going.

Eventually…

Pow!

The Absolute Rock cracked, and my fist pierced through it.

118.
Limitless Recovery Rounds

After the Absolute Rock disappeared, a staircase appeared. Like with Aurum, despite being on the final floor, defeating the rare monster had created a staircase to another floor.

"Looks like it's here," I said.

"What's here?" Emily asked.

"You don't see it, Emily?"

"I don't..."

"What about everyone else?" I asked Celeste, Eve, and Alice. They all shook their heads likewise.

I could see the staircase, so it definitely existed, yet the other four with me couldn't see it.

"Sounds like only I can go down, then. I'm going to meet the spirit of this dungeon. Apparently, people disappear once every few hundred years in each dungeon, I think?"

"Yeah, I've heard about that," the knowledgeable Celeste answered.

The drops in this world could be split into two broad categories: ones that only worked for me, and all others.

Drops outside of dungeons—those of outsiders—only worked for me. Drops inside dungeons, however, worked for everyone.

This staircase was likely the latter if it had appeared for others in the past. My S-rank drops were just what allowed me to get it to appear so quickly.

Perhaps the others couldn't see it because I was the one who'd dealt the killing blow. Whatever the case, that hypothesis satisfied my curiosity for the moment, so I turned around and smiled at my four friends.

"Thanks, everyone. I'll be right back."

"You've got this!" Emily said, prompting agreement from the others.

Encouraged by their cheers, I loaded all kinds of bullets just in case and descended the stairs with their smiles at my back.

At the end of the staircase, I reached an all-white space much like Aurum's. It was even the same in that as soon as I stepped off the staircase, the way back up disappeared.

A single rock lay in the center of it. It looked just like the Absolute Rock I'd just defeated.

"No way... Repetition!"

I cast my all-powerful farming magic. This spell defeated any monster I'd beaten before without exception. The spell hit the rock, but there was no change.

"So it is a different monster, huh?" I muttered to myself, grabbed a gun, and braced myself to fire at any given moment as I approached it. Then, I closed the sixty-foot gap between us.

Fifty... Forty-five, forty, thirty-five, thirty, twenty-five, twenty...

Once I was fifteen feet away, the enemy moved. The rock changed form. Where it had previously sat still like a paperweight, it suddenly began to expand like mad, generating mass out of nowhere. It swelled until, and though still a rock, it had grown to become a seven-foot humanoid.

"A golem, huh?"

A humanoid monster made out of rock, bulky enough to

show that it was a power-type at a glance. Honestly, no word other than golem could describe that as far as I knew. Plus, its shape wasn't all that had changed; unlike every other monster in Arsenic, this one moved and attacked on its own.

It groaned and swung a powerful arm, which I dodged by jumping to the side. Its punch slammed into the ground and shook the room. That would've been bad news if it had hit me.

"How about this?!"

While I evaded, I pointed my barrel and pulled the trigger. First, I used fully-buffed lightning rounds. The bullet drew an electrical path as it flew at the golem.

The golem held out its hand and caught the bullet in its palm. Electricity raged, crackled, and boomed in its hand. Once it subsided, however, the golem was unwounded.

"No good, huh?!"

I evaded his counterattack and tried a few more attacks.

From annihilation rounds to restraining rounds, I used one of everything. And yet, the golem was unmoved.

"So he's as tough as the Absolute Rock, then?"

The sight of it before it transformed came to mind. It was exactly the same as the rare monster that had put us through so much trouble on the floor above.

It probably had the same characteristics. In other words, it was a mobile Absolute Rock.

That's troublesome, but...not that troublesome.

While dodging over and over, I got a good grasp of the golem's abilities.

If its toughness was about equal to S or SS, its strength would be B, while its speed was not even E. It was just an extremely sturdy monster, with little else to it.

B-rank strength was pretty threatening, but it was nothing compared to the defenses of an Absolute Rock. Basically ignorable, honestly.

I stowed my guns and stood in place.

The golem swung its arm for another punch. With all my strength, I punched back. There was a boom as the air shrieked.

Our fists collided, and the golem tottered back. It hadn't taken any damage; it just tottered.

I was becoming more and more certain that it was no threat. It was less powerful than Emily, for all its sturdiness. The only thing special about it was that it moved. And so, I used the same strategy as on the previous floor: I stopped there and punched as hard as I could.

I punched and punched and punched. When the golem attacked, I countered its fist with more punches. It being a counter put more force behind it, so the golem cracked with fewer punches than the Absolute Rock.

It stooped over. I didn't miss this opportunity, showering it with blows. Over and over, I pummeled it with all of my SS-rank strength.

The crack grew, spreading over its body.

Then came the final counter. After that air-shaking blow, the golem began to fall apart. It started with its arm and spread to its body.

Fsssh...

The cluster of rocks sizzled and disappeared.

I watched in silence. After the golem fully faded, a rainbow bullet appeared in its place. I approached and picked it up.

Please choose one limitless bullet.

It was the same as in Aurum. I promptly replied and chose recovery rounds, the one that I'd needed so much more of these days.

The rainbow bullet fused with a recovery round and became limitless.

I loaded it into my gun and fired repeatedly. Countless recovery rounds came out.

"Now I don't have to worry about ever running out of gas for Repetition."

Satisfied by my secondary reward, I put my gun away. And then...

"Well met, young one."

Upon hearing that hoarse voice, I straightened up. I knew that this was where the real challenge would begin.

119.

In a Thousand Years

An old man appeared. He was even smaller than Emily, which meant he was under 4'3". To me, he seemed like an older dwarf or something.

Like with Aurum, he appeared seated like a Jizo statue.

"How many hundreds of years has it been since I was last blessed with a visitor?" he mused.

"Are you Arsenic?"

"The very one. If you already know my name, then might I assume that the surface still has memories of me?"

I only knew this old man was Arsenic because of my past experience with Aurum, but I decided not to mention that. Either way, I had more important business.

"Are you dying?" I asked.

"Indeed I am. Speaking on a human scale… I suppose I have about one month left."

"How can we stop it?"

"It isn't possible for humans."

"I don't care. Tell me how to do it," I insisted.

Arsenic looked at me in surprise. He gazed at me, his eyes searching for my true intent.

After we stared each other down for a while, he said calmly, "Mmm, well, it's no trouble for me to share how, I suppose. Very

well, then. To prolong our lives, we dungeon spirits require Fruit of Life."

"Fruit of Life?"

"You don't know, do you? That is no surprise; it is an illusory fruit unobtainable by human hands. If they could, just touching the legendary fruit would brighten their soul and extend their lifespan."

"Just touching it…extends your lifespan…?"

"Again, human hands—"

"Hold on a second," I cut him off, turned around, and left.

I ran all the way up the stairs to where my friends were waiting in the bloody rain on Arsenic's B30.

"Yoda!" Emily called out.

"How'd it go, Ryota?" Celeste asked.

"Sorry, now isn't the time to explain. Alice, look for the next Absolute Rock for me. I'll have to go down again."

"Okay! Leave it to me," Alice promptly agreed and clenched her fists eagerly.

I turned and ran again, sprinting up the dungeon stairs. I ran out of Arsenic, sped across Cyclo, and dashed into Nihonium.

B1 of Nihonium was, as usual, a skeleton paradise with nobody to farm them.

"Equip the pouch, and… Repetition!"

I equipped my item and used my ultimate farming magic as I rushed through the dungeon.

Once I was done with B1, which I knew like the back of my hand, the pouch was full of HP seeds.

Just touching them prolongs your lifespan. Unobtainable by human hands. I think…he means these.

I took the pouch and left the dungeon, beelining straight for Arsenic.

Back on B30, Celeste awaited me.

"Ryota, this way!"

She led the way. We rounded a few corners and found an Absolute Rock surrounded by the other three.

"Thanks, everyone."

I thanked them all, and they smiled and stepped away from the rock. I then held out my hand and used Repetition—but then, I felt dizzy. That was the feeling of not having enough MP. And so, I whipped out a gun and fired a few limitless recovery rounds into myself.

With my MP fully recovered, I cast Repetition again.

Unsurprisingly for the rare monster of the bottom floor, just one Repetition made me dizzy from the MP loss. However, the path opened once more. We'd struggled against this monster the first time, but since I had beaten it before, Repetition took care of it with ease.

"Yoda, that's incredible!"

"The only person in the world who can do that is Ryota."

"Brazen low level."

"Eve, maybe you should try saying that without blushing?"

"Huh? Eve, are you—?"

My friends clamored over something, but I ignored it for the moment.

After confirming that I had my pouch on hand, I went down the stairs again. The Absolute Rock Golem was there. This one was annoying, too, but I used the same limitless recovery round into Repetition combo to kill it.

Arsenic returned once more.

"Wha—?!" he exclaimed, gazing at me in wide-eyed shock. "You're here again? The same person arriving is a one-in-*billions* chance. Young one, what sort of…?"

"Forget that for now. Are these the Fruit of Life you mentioned?"

"Huh?" Arsenic peeked inside the pouch. His expression was blank at first, but it gradually changed. "Fruit of Life! And so much, too?!"

"So it was this?"

"You… What sort of being are you…?"

"Again, forget it for now. Just use these. I didn't ask how much you needed, so hopefully this is enough. If not, I'll bring more."

"O-Oh, it's…quite enough…"

Arsenic looked befuddled. He still didn't seem to understand what was going on, but his interest was gradually drawn to the HP seeds, so-called Fruit of Life. He took a seed from the pouch—holding it outside Nihonium, like I never could—and put it in his mouth.

After chewing for a bit, he swallowed. His body emitted light.

"I…"

"Yes?"

"I feel rebo-ooorn…"

That sigh was comically long. It was like pent-up gas that had gathered thanks to his patience and the responsibilities forced upon him.

"Delicious… Freakin' delicio-ooous!"

"Your personality really changed on a dime," I chuckled.

"How can you blame me?! This is the first bit of food I've had in a thousand years, and it's freakin' delicio-ooooous!"

Has it been that long? How did he even survive a thousand years without food or water? Is he like a hermit living on air? Or…well, maybe that's why he was dying. He didn't have any food.

Arsenic guzzled down the seeds. Each time he ate, he glowed again. Even I could tell at a glance that his lifespan was growing.

After watching in silence for a moment, I said, "Wait a little longer, pops."

With that, I left him to his rodent-like devouring of the seeds and went back up.

☆

With basket in hand, I returned to Arsenic's space once more. The old man was belching to himself with a big grin on his face, having cleaned up the seeds.

"Hey, young'un. Back again?" he greeted mc with a smile. "You really helped me out. Now I can live on."

"Sure seems like it. The blood rain stopped."

"Right it did. That was a good two hundred years of life."

"That much?"

I hadn't brought that many seeds; it was just one quick lap around Nihonium. I would need ten times that to raise a stat by one rank, yet that was worth two hundred years of life?

"I thank you," he said.

"No problem, but don't you want this?"

"What do you mean?"

"Here," I replied as I held out the basket to the old man. He opened the lid and looked inside. It was full of Emily's home cooking. After leaving before, I'd had Emily cook it for him.

The moment he opened it, the room filled with warmth. Just by existing, Emily's cooking could splash warmth and comfort all around, and it reached even the inhuman old man before me.

The selection of food was all easy-to-eat stuff: rice balls, different sandwiches, and even bite-sized Hamburg steaks. This was an obvious manifestation of Emily's consideration.

He gazed at it blankly for a moment, but the moment it touched his tongue...

"Hooo, man… That's gooooood stuff…"

His reaction was so overt that I didn't know what to say for a moment, but I was just glad that he liked it.

119.5.

My True Desire

I watched in silence as old man Arsenic devoured Emily's food. I'd have felt bad saying something, so I figured I'd wait, except... noticing my gaze, he stopped.

"Sorry about that, son. Lost my self-control there."

"Don't worry about it."

"Still, it's hard to believe the outside world has changed so much in such little time. Who knew food could get this good?"

"This stuff is special, actually," I declared.

"Really!"

The old man's eyes opened wide in surprise.

"My friend Emily made it. Not really my place to brag, but... I'd say that's the most tender flavor in all the world."

"Mmm, I do taste the tender flavor of my mother in it."

How old is this guy's mom? I rebutted mentally. He was a spirit and looked like an old man, so if she did exist, she'd probably be thousands—hell, tens of thousands of years old. *What would the mother of Arsenic be, anyway? Phosphorus? That aside...*

"Say, since you've treated me to such a fine meal, I'll have to thank you somehow," he said.

"You don't really have to."

"I'd be putting my fellow spirits to shame if I didn't."

He aggressively tried to return the favor. Now happy and energetic, he revealed an unexpected stubborn side.

"Is there anything you want?"

"Anything I want…?"

"For example…how about I make it so that when you get flowers from my dungeon, you can give them to someone and get guaranteed sex?"

"That sounds incredible," I mused.

Arsenic was a dungeon that dropped nothing but flowers, and tons of them at that. Getting guaranteed sex just by giving someone flowers from it… Well, that sounded perfect for racy novels. Though, it didn't interest *me* much.

"I'll pass, thanks."

"C'mon, young'un. Already withering at your young age?"

"Not really. There are just things I want more than sex right now."

"Hrmm. Are all people like that these days?"

He looked at me dubiously. Perhaps he was the normal one between us, but I just didn't care much for an ability like that.

"But… I don't really have much else to give you," the old man muttered to himself. He then took onigiri from the basket of Emily's cooking, tore it in half, and held them in both hands.

I watched in silence.

"What's the matter, young'un? Want some?" he asked as he offered one half to me.

"Nah, that's not it. Just thinking about the binary moons."

"Binary moons?"

"Apparently, sometimes two moons appear in the sky, and monsters get stronger and drop more stuff."

He looked down to his hands and his eyes suddenly lit up in understanding.

"Oooh!"

"Wh-What?"

"Riiight, the binary moons."

"Huh?" I mumbled, cocking my head in confusion.

Arsenic tossed both halves of onigiri into his mouth, chewed for only a moment, and swallowed.

You're probably gonna choke...

"Young'un, how about I make it like there are always binary moons in the sky when you're in my dungeon?"

"So there'll always be a drop rate boost?"

"That's right. Whaddya say?"

I thought to myself.

Permanent binary moon effects... There isn't a dungeon that would benefit more from that than Arsenic.

There were two broad traits of the binary moons: drop rates were boosted, and monsters grew stronger.

Arsenic's monsters never attacked. Them being stronger wouldn't change anything, so it was just a flat-out drop rate boost. A permanent binary moon effect sounded incredible.

"So?" he urged.

After a moment's thought, I shook my head and said, "Nah."

"Still doesn't satisfy you, huh? Mmm..."

"No, that's not it. I'd like to ask you for something else," I said as I stared right into his eyes and told him my desire.

He listened to the end and looked back at me with equal parts surprise and exasperation.

"And you really want that?" he confirmed.

"Yeah."

If he could do this, then that was enough for me.

"You're a weird one, young'un. Very well; a worthy reward for delivering the first bit of food I've had in a thousand years."

He smirked and held out his hand, which then glowed, and the shine spread through the dungeon.

And then, the dungeon known as Arsenic...

Afterword

People write novels. Novels are written by people.

Nice to meet you all. Or perhaps, good to see you again. I'm Nazuna Miki, a Taiwanese light novelist.

Thank you so much for picking up volume 4 of *My Unique Skill Makes Me OP Even at Level 1*.

Thanks to you all, we made it to the release of the fourth volume. Also, for the first time in my life, my work has received a manga adaptation! I don't have enough words to express my gratitude, but I truly appreciate all the support!

This volume is similar in essence to the previous three. Conquer dungeons. Make money with drops. Use unique skill and special items to get stronger. On top of that, dungeon spirits have made their first appearance.

By helping these spirits with their troubles, Ryota Sato gains skills that help him per dungeon, honing his strengths in the process.

Feel free to read this volume and find out just how he's growing stronger.

This work continues to be published on *Shousetsuka ni Narou* as well. The web novel doesn't come with illustrations, but it will let you read ahead. It's being updated at a rate of one chapter every two days, and I've gotten 70 million page views now!

If you've read this book and you want more of it right away in Japanese, try Googling it.

Finally, I have many thanks to give.

To Subachi-sama, who continues to make wonderful illustrations.

To K-sama, who continues to edit my awkward writing.

To K Light Novel Books' editorial department, who made this publication a reality.

To the bookstores who stocked this book, and to those of you who bought it.

I offer my deepest thanks to every single person involved in this work.

Here I'll put down my pen, praying that the next volume will someday reach your waiting hands.

Respectfully Yours,

Nazuna Miki
July 2018

Author: Nazuna Miki

Formerly a wannabe voice actor, now a light novelist.
The manga adaptation is tons of fun! Go check it out.

Illustrator: Subachi

Work is a good way to get a fresh look at my art.
I'll do my best to draw more charming characters.